THE NEW PREVENTION OF TERRORISM ACT: THE CASE FOR REPEAL

Updated and expanded third edition covering the extension of the Act in 1984 to cover 'international terrorism'

Catherine Scorer, Sarah Spencer and Patricia Hewitt

National Council for Civil Liberties

National Council for Civil Liberties
21 Tabard Street, London SE1 4LA

© National Council for Civil Liberties 1985

Scorer, Catherine
   The new Prevention of Terrorism Act: the case for repeal. – 3rd
   ed.
   1. Great Britain. Prevention of Terrorism (Temporary
   Provisions) Act 1974   2. Great Britain. Prevention of
   Terrorism (Temporary Provisions) Act 1976 and 1984
   3. Terrorism – Great Britain – Prevention
   I. Title   II. Spencer, Sarah   III. Hewitt, Patricia   IV. Scorer,
   Catherine. Prevention of Terrorism Act   V. National Council
   for Civil Liberties
   344. 105'231   KD8039

   ISBN 0-946088-13-6

Acknowledgements
We should like to thank Dermot Walsh for preparing the chapter
on the operation of the Acts in Northern Ireland; and Lia Dover,
Peter Thornton, Paddy Hillyard and Marie Staunton for their
constructive comments on the draft manuscript.

Typeset, printed and bound in Great Britain by
Yale Press Ltd, London SE25 5LY

Contents

)

Preface

National Council For Civil Liberties

NCCL is unequivocally opposed to the use of violence for political ends: 'terrorism'. We have consistently condemned those who have turned to assassinations and bombings in their desire to change or defend the present constitutional status of Northern Ireland.

Our opposition to violence is in no sense compromised by our opposition to laws such as the Prevention of Terrorism Act which were supposedly introduced to curb terrorist activity. Our position has often been misrepresented by those who believe that criticism of emergency legislation must imply support for those who perpetrate the violence. Nothing could be further from the truth. We oppose emergency legislation because it diminishes the rights of *all* citizens by providing the government, the police and the army with powers unchallengeable in the courts, and by corrupting the standards which are central to the administration of justice. NCCL opposes political violence not only because it threatens the lives of citizens, but because it provides the apparent justification for this drastic curtailment of traditional liberties.

NCCL's concern with emergency legislation in Northern Ireland began in 1936, when we published the report of a Special Commission of Inquiry into the Special Powers Acts.* That report concluded:

> 'First, that through the operation of the Special Powers Acts contempt has been begotten for the representative institutions of government.
> 'Secondly, that through the use of Special Powers individual liberty is no longer protected by law, but is at the arbitrary disposition of the Executive. This abrogation of the rule of law has been so practised as to bring the freedom of the subject into contempt.
>
> 'Thirdly, that the Northern Irish Government has used Special Powers towards securing the domination of one particular

*Report of a Commission of Inquiry into the Special Powers Act (NCCL, 1936; republished 1972). The members of the Commission were Edward Digby KC, JP; Margery Fry, former secretary to the Howard League for Penal Reform; William McKeag, a former Liberal MP and solicitor; Edward Mallalieu MA, a barrister and former Liberal MP. Its secretary was Neil Lawson, later a High Court Judge.

political faction and, at the same time, towards curtailing the lawful activities of its opponents. The driving of legitimate movements underground into illegality, the intimidating or branding as law-breakers of their adherents, however innocent of crime, has tended to encourage violence and bigotry on the part of the Government's supporters as well as to beget in its opponents an intolerance of the 'law and order' thus maintained. The Government's policy is thus driving its opponents into the ways of extremists.'

The experience of the last 50 years and, particularly, of the last 15 years has borne out our contention that emergency powers are *not* a necessary and acceptable response to political violence, but one of the chief causes of continued violence. Denial of civil rights and the implementation of emergency powers feed the conflict from which political violence emerges.

The Prevention of Terrorism Acts of 1974, 1976 and 1984 have destroyed safeguards for the liberty of the individual won over centuries. By replacing legally defined and protected rights with arbitrary executive powers, they have violated cardinal principles of the rule of law. These are strong condemnations. But they are justified by an examination of the extraordinary powers conferred on Ministers by the Acts. NCCL is the only organisation which has monitored in detail the operation of the 1974 and 1976 Acts and it is now monitoring the use of their successor, the 1984 Prevention of Terrorism Act. We hope that, by bringing together information which is not available easily elsewhere, we will alert all those concerned with civil liberties – and in particular, Members of Parliament of all parties – to the dangers inherent in the continued existence of this law.

Introduction

On 21 November 1974, 21 people died following two bomb explosions in Birmingham pubs. Although the alleged perpetrators were apprehended the same day and later convicted, a week of public outcry followed, which included demands for a ban on the IRA, for hanging of convicted terrorists and a new police campaign against the IRA, as well as violent attacks on some Irish people. On 28 November the then Home Secretary, Roy Jenkins, introduced the Prevention of Terrorism (Temporary Provisions) Bill. It was approved by Parliament without a division and came into force the next day.

The Act introduced to Great Britain the emergency legislation which had dominated Northern Ireland for over 50 years. As other reports have shown, the use of repressive legislation exacerbated the violence in Northern Ireland which then spread to the mainland – followed by the emergency legislation which helped create it.

The Prevention of Terrorism Act was based partly on Northern Ireland's Emergency Provisions Act as well as on the Prevention of Violence (Temporary Provisions) Act 1939, introduced in Great Britain in response to an earlier IRA campaign. But it is clear that the details of the 1974 Act had been secretly decided, long before its acceptance by Parliament. Just over 18 months previously – in the aftermath of the Old Bailey bombings of March 1973 – the Home Office, under a Conservative administration, had circulated what were described as 'contingency plans for dealing with terrorism in England'. Several draft Bills were drawn up to proscribe the IRA and to restrict the movement of Irish people from Eire into the UK; in the summer of 1974, the idea of exclusion orders was added to the list of proposals being considered by Government departments.

There were three sections to the Act, the first dealing with the banning of organisations; the second with the exclusion of suspected terrorists at the discretion of the Secretary of State; and the third with the extension of police powers to hold for questioning any person suspected of connection with terrorism. The measures were to last for six months only, although the Act could be renewed – in whole or in part – after that date.

The 1974 Act

From November 1974 to April 1975, NCCL carefully monitored the operation of the Act and published a report which was quoted extensively by MPs during the renewal debate in May 1975. Despite a sharp decline in bombing incidents, in that debate Roy Jenkins recommended a further six-month extension so that the law enforcement agencies would not be left powerless should the bombing campaign resume. But he emphasised the temporary nature of the Act and committed himself to ending it. On 19 May 1975 he said:

> 'I am prepared to tell the House that unless in November I feel able to recommend the dropping of substantial parts of the Act, I shall not ask the House to proceed by order.'

Yet on 28 November 1975 he asked the Commons to do exactly that – while a new Bill published a week previously could pass through its Parliamentary stages.

The new Bill, the basis of the 1976 Act, amended the 1974 Act in three ways. It extended the period within which a person served with an exclusion order could make representations to the Home Office from 48 hours to 96 hours; gave such a person the right to a 'personal interview' with a government nominee; and doubled the lifespan of the Act to one year, after which it could be renewed for up to 12 months an indefinite number of times.

During the three Committee sittings on the Bill (totalling about eight hours discussion) the Conservative MPs and Enoch Powell MP (Official Unionist Party) were particularly vociferous, and amendments which stiffened and extended the Bill were later incorporated with Government agreement. Demands for compulsory identity cards and the reintroduction of hanging were, however, resisted.

The important changes later ratified by the Commons made it an offence not to pass on to the police information about terrorism, widened the provisions relating to financial and political support for proscribed organisations and provided for exclusion from Northern Ireland back to Great Britain. Amendments tabled on the floor of the Commons to abolish exclusion orders and to give the Judges' Rules statutory force were thrown out. The Act as amended became law on 25 March 1976.

The 1976 Act

With minor amendments, this Act remained in force until March 1984.

In December 1977 an inquiry headed by Lord Shackleton was established to report on the operation of the Act. Its terms of reference were as follows:

> *Accepting the continuing need for legislation against terrorism,* to assess the operation of the Prevention of Terrorism (Temporary Provisions) Acts 1974 and 1976, with particular reference to the effectiveness of this legislation and its effects on the liberties of the subject. (our italics)

Thus, the inquiry excluded consideration of the need for 'emergency' legislation of this type. His recommendations, published in August 1978, (Cmnd 7324) can be summarised as follows:

— statistics on the operation of the Act should be published quarterly;
— exclusion order cases should be reviewed with the possibility of the orders being revoked;
— the government should reconsider its policy on financial assistance to relatives of excluded persons;
— section 11 (withholding information) should be allowed to lapse;
— improvements should be made in the diet and comfort of detainees;
— the Judges' Rules should be uniformly followed;
— fullest possible records of interviews should be kept;
— detention at ports should be for the same maximum period as elsewhere, i.e. seven days, not 12.

On 18 June 1979, the Home Secretary announced that exclusion orders would be reviewed after three years if the excluded person so wished. Those who were eligible and whose addresses were known to the Home Office were then approached. Since that date, detailed quarterly statistics on the operation of the Act have been produced by both the Home Office and the Northern Ireland Office.

On police advice, the Government subsequently refused to allow Section 11 to lapse and turned down Lord Shackleton's suggestion that financial assistance be given to relatives on the grounds that 'such a scheme could not be justified' (statement by the Home Secretary, 1980).

The Prevention of Terrorism (Supplemental Temporary Provisions) Amendment Order 1979 was also agreed on 21 March 1979. From 18 April 1979 the length of time the police could detain a person at a port or airport on their own authority was reduced to 48 hours in line with their powers of detention elsewhere, the authority of the Secretary of State being required for an extension for a further five days.

On 3 July 1979, the Irish National Liberation Army was added to the schedule of proscribed organisations following their claim of responsibility for the assassination of a leading Conservative MP, Airey Neave.

The only other amendment involved a procedural change. In the renewal debate of 4 March 1980, the Home Secretary, stated that a new direction, to come into force on 25 March 1980, would enable an excluded person to be held for a further 24 hours beyond the seven days in police custody if arrangements were being made for his or her removal within that time. This, he said, was designed to prevent an excluded person from being transferred to prison from a police cell unnecessarily.

The 1984 Act

The 1976 Act was renewed annually by successive governments with the agreement of the opposition parties until 1982. In March of that year, the parliamentary consensus was finally broken when the Labour Opposition abstained in the vote to renew the Act. In response, the Government set up a new inquiry into the operation of the Act to be conducted by Lord Jellicoe, a former Conservative minister. His terms of reference, like those of Lord Shackleton, restricted his inquiry by *accepting the continuing need for legislation against terrorism.*

Lord Jellicoe's report was published in February 1983 (Cmnd 8803). He recommended that the Act should be retained and that parts of it – the powers of arrest and detention – should be extended to cover those suspected of involvement in 'international terrorism'. Recognising that the impact of the Act, 'actual and potential, upon our civil liberties is so great', he also recommended certain minor amendments to enhance parliamentary control over the Act and mitigate the effect of its powers.

In July 1983, the Government published a Bill to implement most of Lord Jellicoe's recommendations. The following chart shows Lord Jellicoe's key recommendations and whether they were incorporated in the new Bill (which subsequently became the 1984 Act):

Lord Jellicoe's Key Recommendations	*Incorporated in Bill*
The Act: 'Temporary Provisions' should be removed from the short title of the Act. It should continue to require annual renewal but have a maximum life of 5 years. Any further counter-terrorism legislation should require a new Bill.	**YES** (But an amendment proposed by Enoch Powell MP to reinstate the term won government support and the Act once again became the Prevention of Terrorism (*Temporary Provisions*) Act.

Extension of Police Powers: Power to arrest someone suspected of involvement in terrorism should be extended to include suspected international terrorists (but not those suspected of domestic terrorism unconnected with Northern Ireland)

YES

The power to detain terrorist suspects at ports should similarly be extended to international terrorism.

YES

Detention: Police applications to detain a suspect beyond 48 hours (without charge) should be approved by the Home Secretary personally.

NO

The Home Secretary should be able to extend the detention by any period between 0 and 5 days.

YES

Officers at ports have the right to detain anyone without suspicion, for up to 12 hours, after which they should have 'reasonable suspicion'.

NO
(But this provision was subsequently included in a 'supplemental order' to the Act which has the force of law).

Access to a solicitor: Suspects should have an absolute right to see a solicitor after 48 hours' detention.

NO
(But a qualified right for suspects held under the PTA to see a solicitor after 48 hours was included in the Police and Criminal Evidence Act see below).

Notification of a Friend: Suspects should *not* have an absolute right to have a friend or relative notified of their arrest if police think this would interfere with the investigation.

YES

Exclusion: British citizens resident in one part of the UK for 3 years (instead of 20) should not be liable to exclusion from it.

YES

The time period during which a person subject to an exclusion order is entitled to make representations against the order should be extended from 96 hours to 7 days.

YES

Withholding information: Section 11 should remain in force but no longer carry a power of arrest under this Act.   YES

It should be made clear in the Act that Section 11 relates only to third parties and does not oblige the suspect to incriminate him or herself.   YES

The first Parliamentary debate on the Bill, the Second Reading in the House of Commons, was on 24 October 1983. The Labour Opposition officially opposed the whole Bill and attempted to vote down or amend it at every stage of its passage through Parliament, but without success.

The only opposition amendment to receive majority support was that from Enoch Powell MP restoring 'Temporary Provisions' to the title of the Bill. A series of Government amendments clarified its wording and in one case, Clause 10, extended its powers. In response to considerable lobbying against the extension of the detention powers to cover international terrorist suspects, the Home Secretary promised to issue a circular to the police advising them to restrict their use of these powers. (See Arrest and Detention). In the House of Lords, an Independent peer persuaded the Government to appoint a 'Commissioner' to examine the operation of the Act each year and to report to both Houses of Parliament before each renewal debate. The Bill was debated for a total of 37 hours in the House of Commons and nearly 11 hours in the House of Lords. It came into force on 22 March 1984 and its Supplemental Temporary Provisions Order on 27 March 1984.

NCCL's objections to the Act

The Government originally justified the 1974 Act, described by the then Home Secretary as 'draconian' and 'unprecedented in peacetime', on the grounds that a panic-stricken country would take the law into its own hands unless the Government stepped in. It was sold to a willing Parliament as a temporary expedient – an Act with built-in obsolescence which would automatically lapse unless emergency conditions justified renewal. The emergency nature of the legislation has now been largely forgotten – not least by the police – and the failure of a concerted campaign to repeal the Act has meant that it has, in practice, become an integral part of our criminal law.

Ten years experience of the operation of the Acts has more than justified NCCL's initial opposition. The basic objections to the powers given to the Home Secretary and the police – the executive arm of government – may be summarised as follows.

In the United Kingdom, where the rights of citizens are not protected by a Bill of Rights, Parliamentary scrunity and judicial review provide the only methods of preserving civil liberties in an emergency. But the 1974 Bill was rushed through all its Parliamentary stages in two days without any pretence of full and thorough scrutiny of its provisions. The 1976 Act doubled the period of renewal from six to 12 months, and renewal debates on both Acts have generally been brief and ill-attended.

Powers cannot be challenged in court

Secondly, by giving the Home Secretary and the police powers which cannot be challenged in the courts, the Prevention of Terrorism Acts have destroyed at a stroke the edifice of safeguards built up in this country's legal system to protect the citizen against wrongful arrest, detention or conviction. Exclusion is identical in many essential respects to the discredited power to intern without trial: it allows the police, where they have no evidence on which to prosecute, to apply for an *executive* order against the suspect. The Home Secretary is given the unlimited power to decide – in secret and on the basis of evidence never made known to the suspects, their lawyers or the public – whether or not they are in fact involved in political violence. Thus, vital features of the rule of law – the right to know the charges, the right to hear and challenge the evidence, the right to a fair hearing and the right of appeal – are abolished. The open decision of a court has been replaced by the secret decision of the police, civil servants and a Minister. The inevitable result is that innocent people are deprived of their freedom on evidence which would never stand up to the scrutiny of a court of law.

Excessive powers open to abuse

NCCL predicted in 1974 that the existence of the new police powers combined with public pressure against Irish Republican sympathisers would lead the police to indulge in 'fishing trips' which would waste police manpower, result in few criminal convictions and harden attitudes. And the *Daily Mail* stated:

> The net effect of these special powers as far as the police are concerned is that they will be freer to harry, harass and interrogate terrorist suspects and terrorist sympathisers.

Now after each incident, such as the murder of Airey Neave and

Lord Mountbatten, or the Harrod's bomb, mass arrests under the Prevention of Terrorism Act are made and widely reported, although many of those detained are in fact not connected or involved with the crime which served as the pretext for their detention. The ordinary criminal law, which requires the suspect to be arrested on reasonable suspicion of an offence, gives the police more than adequate powers to bring suspects against whom there is real evidence to court: the Prevention of Terrorism Act, on the other hand, allows the police to arrest, detain and interrogate those against whom there is no evidence at all.

Shift in the burden of proof

Central to the English legal system is the principle that a person is innocent until proved guilty. But repeatedly under this Act it is the innocent person who must establish his or her case. Those who have been detained and *released without charge* – the vast majority of those held under the Act – are frequently referred to by Home Secretaries as 'terrorists', while the records held on them by the police ensure that having once been detained and released they will again become objects of entirely unjustifiable suspicion. Someone faced with an exclusion order is offered the almost impossible task of persuading the Home Secretary and his advisers that the accusations against them – of which they know nothing – are unfounded. The attitude amongst supporters of the Acts seems to be that this shift in the burden of proof is unimportant – after all, 'innocent people have nothing to fear'. The reality is that for 'innocent' one should read 'non-Irish, not involved or interested in Irish politics, does not live, work or mix socially with Irish people, does not read literature concerning Ireland, does not belong to a political party or other body which might be critical of British Government policy in Ireland'.

Counterproductive

The experience of emergency powers in Northern Ireland has demonstrated that mass searches, arrests for interrogation, detentions to obtain confessions and internment without trial have been counterproductive in combating violence. The effect has been to harden attitudes amongst both communities. In ending the use of the internment power, the Government itself acknowledged that executive powers which further undermined confidence in the institutions of the law could actually contribute to the violence which they were designed to counter. If the Prevention of Terrorism Act were used for the detention and exclusion of Irish people living in Britain on a larger scale – the result could well be a renewed spiralling of violence. The injustices which the operation of the Acts have so far caused in their use against the Irish community in Britain have already led to fear and alienation amongst ordinary, law-abiding families.

Emergency Powers become permanent

A further danger of 'emergency powers' is that they become permanent. The 1922 Special Powers Acts, for example, became permanent in 1933, and remained in force in Northern Ireland until replaced by the Emergency Provisions Act in 1973. The 1939 Prevention of Violence (Temporary Provisions) Act stayed on the statute book for 15 years. The 1973 Emergency Provisions (Northern Ireland) Act (now the 1978 Act) has now been with us 12 years, and the Prevention of Terrorism Act itself for 11 years.

Moves to abolish the right to silence, to increase the period within which suspects can be held without charge or to reduce the right to jury trial are significantly strengthened when these measures are already in existence in emergency legislation. Until 1974 the maximum period for which suspects could usually be detained without charge was 48 hours. Under the PTA, this period was extended to 7 days. In 1983 the Government introduced its Police and Criminal Evidence Bill which increased the period many suspects can be held to 96 hours: 4 days. When Lord Jellicoe reviewed the PTA (many months before the new Police Bill was enacted), his recommendation that the 7-day period should remain was in turn influenced, he said, by the provisions, in the new Police Bill because his guiding principle was that 'the powers available to deal with terrorism should differ as little as possible from those in the general law.'

Effect of the new international provisions

The 1984 Act has only been in force for a few months at the time of writing. It is not yet possible therefore to assess the impact of the extension of its detention provisions (which previously related only to those suspected of involvement in terrorism connected with Northern Ireland) to cover international terrorist suspects. The wording of the Act allows the police and port officials to detain anyone suspected of involvement in political violence anywhere in the world whether or not it has any connection with the UK. NCCL warned MPs during the passage of the Bill that the powers could be used to harass and detain foreigners – students, refugees or supporters of liberation movements overseas – in order to obtain information from them, although they were not suspected of committing any offence in this country. The British Council of Refugees said:

> 'Most people granted asylum in the UK have fled brutal and repressive regimes. Clause 12 of the Bill is drafted in such a way that refugees who have fled from countries where people are held incommunicado for long periods or who have false charges brought against them may find themselves detained incommunicado in the UK, the country where they have sought refuge . . . The United Kingdom has a long tradition of providing refuge to those fleeing repressive regimes. We therefore urge you to amend this Bill, to ensure that its powers cannot be used against any refugee or asylum seeker living peacefully in this country, and that it should not be retroactive.'

During the debate on this clause of the Bill Lord Shackleton told the House of Lords: 'The concern is that people who might be fleeing from oppressive governments . . . might not know whether they can come here safely or whether they will be picked up.'

Terrorism and civil liberties

Supporters of the Act argue that civil liberties must be sacrificed to deal with those suspected of terrorism. They are wrong. First, it is not necessary to introduce excessive powers which infringe civil liberties when the ordinary criminal law provides the police with wide powers to arrest and detain anyone suspected of a terrorist offence. The small percentage of those arrested under the Act and later charged with a criminal offence could and should have been arrested under normal, pre-existing police powers and brought before a court in the usual way. Secondly, it is just as important that the rights of someone suspected of a terrorist offence are respected as those of someone suspected of a non-political offence. Indeed, given the overwhelming horror which juries and judges rightly feel when dealing with terrorist crimes, safeguards for the suspect are arguably even more important than in lesser cases.

The exclusion procedure, abolishing all safeguards, immeasurably increases the risk that an innocent person will be punished. The long periods of detention before charge, with the consequent possibility of false confession and wrongful conviction, is not only an injustice to the innocent person, but means that the guilty person often goes free.

In NCCL's view, the PTA infringes the European Convention of Human Rights, to which the UK is a signatory. The Convention permits governments to 'derogate' from most of its provisions during an emergency and the British Government entered a notice of derogation for the Emergency Provisions Act (until it withdrew it in 1984). But it has taken the view that the PTA does not infringe the Convention. NCCL has challenged this view by representing a number of people arrested or excluded under the Act in cases under the Convention, as yet without success.

In our view, the Act infringes Article 5 (the right to liberty), Article 6 (the right to a fair hearing), Article 8 (respect for private and family life), Articles 10 and 11 (freedom of expression and assembly) and Article 14 (prohibiting discrimination in the protection of these rights on grounds of national origin). The few cases that have been taken to the European Commission of Human Rights are referred to in the relevant chapters below.

Banned Organisations

What the Act says

The Prevention of Terrorism Act gives the Secretary of State the power to ban an organisation which 'appears' to him to be concerned with terrorism in any part of the United Kingdom, relating to Northern Irish affairs. In relation to the *banning* of organisations, the powers in the 1984 Act are identical to those in the 1976 Act.

The Irish Republican Army was the only banned organisation specified in the 1974 Act and it has remained banned ever since. On 3 July 1979, the Irish National Liberation Army – which had claimed responsibility for the murder of Airey Neave – was also banned. No other organisations are banned under the Act.

'Terrorism' is defined as the use of violence for political ends and includes any use of violence for the purpose of putting the public or any section of the public in fear.

A person may not:

(i) belong to a proscribed organisation;
(ii) raise or receive money or goods on behalf of a proscribed organisation;
(iii) encourage any other form of support for a proscribed organisation;
(iv) organise a public or private meeting of more than two people in support of a proscribed organisation;
(v) organise a public or private meeting addressed by a member of a proscribed organisation, even if he or she is addressing the meeting on something unconnected with Northern Ireland affairs.

Maximum penalties are on conviction in a magistrates' court, a fine of £2,000 and/or six months' imprisonment, of if the case is heard in a Crown Court, an unlimited fine and/or five years' imprisonment. The court may also forfeit any money and goods held for a proscribed organisation.

A person is not guilty of membership of a proscribed organisation if all his or her activities in it took place before it was proscribed. But it is up to the defendant to prove this.

It is an offence to display, carry or wear in public anything which arouses a reasonable apprehension that you are a member or supporter of a proscribed organisation – even if you are not. Maximum penalties for this are a fine of £2,000 and/or six months' imprisonment: these cases may only be heard in the magistrates' court.

In addition to these offences, Section 10 of the 1976 Act also created a number of offences which relate to support for 'terrorism' in general, rather than to support for a proscribed organisation. Someone who knew or suspected that his or her money or goods were being used in connection with the 'commission, preparation or instigation' of acts of terrorism *in the UK,* connected with Northern Irish affairs, could be charged with an offence regardless of whether he or she was connected with a banned organisation.

The 1984 Act (as a result of a government amendment to its own Bill) extended this power by removing the words 'in the UK'. In other words, the offence is committed if the act of terrorism to which the offence refers takes place *in the UK or anywhere in the world* if it is connected with Northern Ireland.

Under Section 10 it is an offence to:

(i) ask for a gift or loan which is intended to be used in connection with terrorism connected with Northern Ireland;
(ii) receive or accept any money or other goods intended to be used in this connection;
(iii) give or lend, or make available in any other way, any money or goods, knowing or suspecting it will be used in this connection.

The offences themselves must be committed within the UK. The penalties are the same as for the offences relating to banned organisations. For any of these offences, a suspect can be arrested and detained without a warrant.

The record

Only one person was charged and convicted for support of a proscribed organisation under the 1974 Act. He was James Fegan, of Glasgow, convicted in February 1975 of soliciting support for the IRA by offering posters for sale. He had allegedly been heard in a bar asking drinkers whether they wanted to buy a poster to 'support the boys'. He had not sold any of the posters. He was sentenced to six months' imprisonment. Two others – Gerald McMorrow and William McGuigan – charged at the same time as Fegan were acquitted.

Up until 31 December 1984 a total of ten people were charged in Great Britain with offences relating to proscription. Seven people were charged with soliciting or receiving money for a proscribed organisation, of whom five were acquitted and two received prison sentences of less than a year. Three people were charged with displaying support for a proscribed organisation: two of the cases were dropped and the third person was found guilty and fined.

Of the total of 161 people who have ever been prosecuted under the Acts (up to 31 December 1984) 62 (39%) were charged under Section 10 of whom 39 were convicted.

Six people were found guilty of soliciting money for use in acts of terrorism; ten of receiving money or property for use in acts of terrorism; fifteen people for soliciting and receiving; and four people for soliciting and/or giving money or property for such use. A further four people were charged and convicted under Section 10 who had not originally been detained under the Act. Of the 62 people originally charged under Section 10, ten cases were not proceeded with, 39 were convicted and thirteen acquitted. 29 received sentences of up to five years and ten received five or more years.

In August 1980, two members of the Revolutionary Communist Group were arrested for selling papers allegedly in support of the Provisional IRA and were charged with displaying items in public which could give rise to an apprehension that they were members of a proscribed organisation. The charge was later replaced by a charge of soliciting financial support for a proscribed organisation and the defendants were remanded *in custody* for a week. At the trial, however, the Prevention of Terrorism Act charge was dropped completely – and replaced by breach of the peace.

In December 1983 a Sinn Fein official, Jan Taylor, was arrested in a London pub by officers of the Metropolitan Police Special Branch. He was charged under Section 2 of the Act with selling the '1984 Republican Resistance Calendar' in circumstances likely to arouse reasonable apprehension that he was a supporter of a proscribed organisation, the IRA. The calendar contained photographs of IRA paramilitaries and Republican commemorative dates, and referred to the killing of Lord Mountbatten as an 'execution'. His defence counsel reportedly argued, at his trial in May 1984, that the calendar was on sale in Collet's London Bookshop and that Mr Taylor was selling Republicanism not enlisting support for the IRA in particular. Mr Taylor was convicted by the magistrate and fined £150.

The effect of bans

Proscription has inevitably led to the curtailing of debate and legitimate political activity by groups campaigning peacefully on Irish matters. The passing of the Act created an unease – in part justified – that a person could be charged for beliefs rather than criminal activity. The form of words used blurs the distinction between members of a banned organisation and Republican or Loyalist sympathisers. After November 1974 both Provisional Sinn Fein and Clann na h'Eireann, which were pursuing political campaigns for similar objectives to those of the Provisional and Official IRA respectively, restricted their political activity for fear of a charge under the Act. The atmosphere at that time can be gauged from press reports that people were afraid to be associated with anything Irish. Even Irish harps had apparently been destroyed.

NCCL has been consulted by many different groups on issues which range from the selling of Easter Lilies (which commemorate the Rising of 1916 in Dublin) to raising money for prisoners' families and selling newspapers. It certainly appeared that the selling of Republican papers was an invitation for an arrest and interrogation under the Act by the police. During 1979, for instance, five supporters of 'Hands Off Ireland' (a campaign organised by the Revolutionary Communist Group) were arrested.

It was clear at an early stage in the operation of the 1974 Act that the bans themselves were not of major importance. Both the Home Office and the police had argued against a ban on the IRA until after the Birmingham bombings, when the ban was said to be necessary to placate public opinion. The real value of the ban, in the eyes of the authorities, was that it allowed a wide range of activities unconnected with criminal offences to be curtailed. Ian Gilmour MP, who was spokesman for the Conservative Party during the 1974 debate on the Act, confirmed his party's view when he said in that debate: 'I think, too, that it has cut down the activities of both the political wings of both the Provisional and Official IRA, and that also is to the good.' The same party has (rightly in NCCL's view) rejected calls for a ban on the National Front or its political activities on the grounds that, however objectionable their views, democracy demands that they be allowed to exist.

In 1976, when the new Bill was introduced, the Home Secretary was unperturbed by the fact that the section concerning banned organisations had then, as now, hardly been used – producing one conviction in 16 months. He argued that it was preventive in intention, the absence of convictions being a sign of success! Lord Jellicoe, in his inquiry, found that he had some sympathy with the criticism that banning an organisation is an unacceptable infringement of freedom of speech and that its members should, instead, be prosecuted for any criminal offences which they commit. But the arguments against proscription, he said, are not necessarily the same as those in favour of abolishing the power once it exists. To do so would imply that the government had changed its attitude to these organisations and would provoke a wave of public resentment. When the power was first introduced, he said, it was considered one of the Act's most important provisions: 'I believe that time has proved this judgement to be mistaken' he wrote; but proscription had reduced the public display of support for the organisations and 'I conclude, therefore, that proscription had some – albeit relatively limited – beneficial effects.'

Against the bans

Membership of an illegal organisation is difficult to prove, unless admitted. In Northern Ireland, a refusal of members of paramilitary organisations to recognise the court is usually taken as an admission of guilt. Most of those charged with 'membership' in Northern Ireland are also charged with a more serious offence, so that if the judge acquits the defendant of the heavier offence, the membership charge acts as a net to ensure conviction.

Proscription has been rejected in the past on the basis that the police considered it would make detection more difficult. Roy Jenkins made it clear, when introducing the ban, that proscription itself would not reduce terrorism. Previous Home Secretaries had refused to consider proscription on the grounds that new organisations with the same aims and methods would emerge under a different name or that activities and supporters would disappear underground, hampering the surveillance work of the police.

Lord Shackleton in his report stated that proscription of the IRA had not, in the view of the police, made more than a marginal contribution to the curtailment of the activities of the IRA, and the justification for it did not derive principally from its 'operational' value. Lord Jellicoe, as we have seen, thought the power had only 'some, albeit relatively limited, beneficial effect'.

The only argument which supporters of proscription can put forward is that public opinion would be affronted if this part of the Act were allowed to lapse. The Home Secretary acknowledged, during the passage of the 1983 Bill, that 'it is dangerous to proscribe organisations, it is not something that anyone wants to do and . . . I regard it as an unusual and disagreeable action which is not routine'. However, he continued, '. . . when people are being, and have been, killed in the cause of terrorism, it is intolerable to expect their friends, neighbours and relations to stand by while the organisation that has done it is parading before them in the streets'.

By its nature, proscription is arbitrary. The Act allows the Secretary of State to ban an organisation 'if it appears' to him to be involved in terrorism connected with Northern Irish affairs. There is no enquiry. Evidence need not be produced. No appeal is permitted by the organisation banned. There is no Parliamentary debate. The choice of the word 'appears' is designed deliberately to exclude judicial review. The Minister's decision can only be challenged if it can be *proved* that he acted in bad faith, an impossible burden to discharge.

The full potential of the power to ban has been recognised by the police. In a pamphlet published by Police Review Publications, entitled *Public Order and the Police*, the following appeared:

> A much simpler action to prevent any of our present troubles would be to declare the National Front, the Socialist Workers' Party or whatever party is causing trouble to be a proscribed organisation under the Prevention of Terrorism (Temporary Provisions) Act 1976.

The pamphlet was written by Kenneth Sloan, training officer with the Manchester Police, and carried an introduction by William Whitelaw, now Deputy Leader of the Conservative Party.

As Martin Flannery MP said in the 1980 renewal debate: 'There is a spirit of witch hunt and retribution calling for the proscription of groups that have nothing proven against them under the Act.'

There is no doubt that many people in Northern Ireland, as in Great Britain, find Republican views offensive – just as many people find the views of Loyalists and Orange Order members offensive. The Act has not prevented the publication and distribution in Northern Ireland of Republican newspapers which describe members of the Provisional IRA as freedom fighters and attacks on civilians and soldiers as victories. Nor has it prevented the expression of extreme Orange views. The literature which has led to prosecutions under the Act in Great Britain is in fact far less 'offensive' than much which is freely obtainable in Northern Ireland. The effect of the Act is simply to restrict even further the range of opinions available to those people in Britain interested in the situation in Northern Ireland.

The central point is that no organisation should be banned and no publication censored simply because it is offensive. The freedoms of association and expression, which are fundamental to political activity in a democracy, involve the right to make one's views known and to organise with others of a similar conviction. It is inevitable that some views expressed in a democracy will be deeply objectionable to others. They will also be deeply objectionable to those in authority, who are inevitably tempted to respond, not to the arguments or views expressed, but by banning the organisation or prosecuting the individuals involved.

Moreover, a brief examination of the history of Northern Ireland shows just how futile bans are. The ban on the IRA and other organisations under the Emergency Provisions Act has not prevented the organisations from existing. Nor has the ban diminished support for their views. The various means used by the British Government within Great Britain itself to curtail the expression of different points of view about Northern Ireland have on the other hand helped ensure that the British public has little or no understanding of the situation in that part of the country and that the Government can take almost any measures without serious debate or opposition. That policy of censorship has not helped the British Government achieve security or peace in Northern Ireland; it has seriously undermined democratic freedoms throughout the whole of the United Kingdom; and it has left the public, most MPs and most of the press utterly complacent about the measures which it is right for a Government to take in dealing with opposition.

In its report on offences against the person, published in March 1980, the Criminal Law Revision Committee rejected a proposal to make terrorism as such a criminal offence. It is easy to see why the Committee was right. 'Terrorism' is incapable of a precise definition, as the Prevention of Terrorism Act itself illustrates. Terrorist *activities* are already in themselves criminal offences. If terrorism itself is not an offence, it is wrong in our view to make 'support for terrorism', as in Section 10, a crime. Any support for criminal activity, whether involving terrorists or anyone else, should be prosecuted under the general law of incitement or conspiracy or more especially for substantive offences.

Exclusion orders

What the Act says

Under this part of the Act, it is important to remember that Great Britain means England, Scotland and Wales; United Kingdom means Great Britain and Northern Ireland.

Under the Act, any Secretary of State – it will usually be the Home Secretary or Northern Ireland Secretary – can decide to make an exclusion order against a person if:

(i) it appears to him expedient, in order to prevent acts of terrorism intended to influence Government policy or public opinion with respect to Northern Ireland affairs, *and*
(ii) he believes that a person is or has been concerned in the 'commission, preparation or instigation, of acts of terrorism', *or*
(iii) he believes that a person is attempting to enter Great Britain or Northern Ireland, with a view to being concerned in the commission, preparation or instigation of acts of terrorism.

The powers in the 1984 Act are almost identical to those in the 1976 Act: the only differences concern the definition of those liable to exclusion and the rights of someone subject to an exclusion order to make representations to the Secretary of State.

'Terrorism' is defined as the use of violence for political ends and includes any use of violence for the purpose of putting the public or any section of the public in fear. The definition is wide enough to include violence with almost any connection, however remote, with political motives.

UK citizens

If a person is a United Kingdom citizen they cannot be excluded from the United Kingdom completely. But they can be restricted to living either in Northern Ireland or in Great Britain.

A UK citizen can be excluded from Great Britain to Northern Ireland:

(i) unless they have ordinarily been resident in Great Britain throughout the last three years (not including time spent in prison in the United Kingdom, Channel Isles or Isle of Man); or

(ii) unless they have already been excluded from Northern Ireland.

A person similarly can be excluded from Northern Ireland to Great Britain:

(i) unless they have been ordinarily resident in Northern Ireland throughout the last three years; or
(ii) unless they have already been excluded from Great Britain.

If a person objects to an exclusion order on any of these grounds, it is up to them to prove their case.

Citizens of other countries

A citizen of a foreign country can be excluded from the United Kingdom altogether and can be sent to the country they are most closely connected with.

The exclusion procedure

A United Kingdom citizen subject to an exclusion order is usually removed from Great Britain to Northern Ireland and is prohibited from entering Great Britain or being there. As we have seen the Act also permits someone to be excluded *from* Northern Ireland to Britain, but this power is rarely used. No UK citizen can be excluded from both Northern Ireland and Great Britain.

A citizen of a foreign country who is excluded is prohibited from entering or being in any part of the United Kingdom.

The excluded person can make representations against exclusion within seven days of notice being served and also has a right to request an oral hearing before a government Adviser. In 1985, the Advisers were Sir Brian Bailey OBE JP (chairman of the South West Regional Health Authority and of Television South West Ltd); Henry Brooke QC and Hugh Carlisle QC. If the excluded person has agreed to leave and has been removed before the expiry of that period, he or she may exercise these rights to make representations within fourteen days of their removal.

If an individual makes representations, the Secretary of State must refer the case to one of the Advisers. Those excluded persons who make representations before they are removed have a right to a personal interview with the Adviser. Those who have already left will be granted an interview if the Secretary of State thinks it is 'practicable'. (This caveat is to remove from the Secretary of State a duty to provide such an interview, at great expense, to an excluded person removed to a distant foreign country). The interview is private and the individual has no right to have a lawyer present. The person is given no information about why he or she is being excluded.

The Secretary of State has a duty under the Act to take into account the representations made by the excluded person, the report of any interview with the Adviser and the Adviser's opinion. He must then notify the person in writing of his decision whether or not to revoke the order.

If a person is served with an exclusion order, they are normally transferred from police custody to prison seven days after arrest. A person may be held in police custody for a further 24 hours (eight days in all) while arrangements are being made for their removal – if they consent to removal or have chosen not to make representations.

A person subject to an exclusion order has no right:

— to know the evidence on which the exclusion order is made;
— to cross-examine on the evidence;
— to have a public or formal hearing;
— to know on what basis the representations were successful or unsuccessful;
— to appeal to a court or tribunal against exclusion.

An exclusion order can be revoked at any time by the Secretary of State and will expire automatically after three years. The fact that an exclusion order has been revoked or expired does not prevent the Secretary of State making a further order against the person. An exclusion order made under the 1974 or 1976 Act will, unless revoked earlier, expire at the end of three years *after* the date of enactment of the current 1984 Act: i.e. in March 1987. (Section 18(2))

Detention at ports of entry

Under the Act, if a person is entering or leaving Great Britain or Northern Ireland (including people coming in as transit passengers), he or she can be detained at the port of entry, while the Secretary of State decides if he wants to make an exclusion order. The person can be detained by any 'examining officer' – i.e. a police officer, an immigration officer or a customs officer working as an immigration officer (and, in the case of Northern Ireland only, a soldier). The Government has given an undertaking that a person subject to an exclusion order, in transit at a United

Kingdom port, will not be deemed to have broken his or her exclusion order.

A person can be detained for 48 hours and then for another five days on the authority of the Secretary of State pending a decision whether or not to make an exclusion order. (See Arrest and Detention)

Committing a criminal offence

Under Section 9 of the Act, it is a criminal offence:

(i) not to obey an exclusion order once notice has been served;
(ii) to help any person who is known or ought to be known to be subject to an exclusion order, to enter the country against the order;
(iii) to harbour a person who is subject to an exclusion order.

For any of these offences a person may be arrested without a warrant although the Attorney General must give his consent before prosecution. Maximum penalty on conviction in the magistrates' court is a £2,000 fine and/or six months' imprisonment; in the Crown Court an unlimited fine and/or five years' imprisonment.

The record in Great Britain

Between 29 November 1974 and 31 December 1984, 358 applications for an exclusion order were made, of which 48 were refused by the Home Secretary, 11 orders were revoked before the person was removed, and 54 others were revoked after the person had been removed. Of these 65 revocations, 15 were revoked following representations (out of a total of 44 contested orders); 43 following a review of 77 orders, which had been in force for three years (6 of these cases were still being considered); 7 'for other reasons'. Of the 310 exclusion orders made, 206 were made against a person detained at a port or airport and 69 against a person detained elsewhere. 35 were made against a person not detained under the Act. 245 excluded persons were returned to Northern Ireland, 40 to the Republic of Ireland. Thirteen were already outside Great Britain when the order was made. Thirty people were excluded from Northern Ireland, 11 of them in 1981.

Fourteen people have been charged in Great Britain for failing to comply with an exclusion order, of whom 11 were found guilty. (Two cases were not proceeded with and one was awaiting trial).

Of those found guilty, four were fined, one received a suspended sentence and six were imprisoned for one year or less. Four people were charged with helping an excluded person to breach an order of whom three were found guilty. Two were fined, one was imprisoned for a year or less. (One case was not proceeded with).

In Northern Ireland, eight people were charged during this period with failing to comply with an exclusion order.

Exclusion orders revoked

Of the 44 people who had made representations against an exclusion order up to the end of December 1984 only 15 had their order revoked. Very few people challenge the order: not because they admit their guilt but because they are unwilling to remain in prison for several days or weeks awaiting a final decision or are reluctant to submit themselves to the farcical procedures involved in making representations.

Following a recommendation of Lord Shackleton, the Home Secretary began to review exclusion orders which had been in force for three years. The excluded person asking for a review is required to complete a form giving details of all home addresses and employers since exclusion. By the end of December 1984 97 people had asked for a review of their exclusion order: 43 orders were revoked and 48 confirmed.

How exclusion orders work

Within an hour of the 1974 Act coming into operation, Scotland Yard presented the Home Secretary with a file containing the names of alleged IRA activists whom it wanted excluded from the country. The first applications were all made by the Special Branch and were reportedly accompanied by documentary evidence indicating the involvement of those people named. The list of excluded persons was then issued to the press by the Home Office.

The exclusion order gives no reasons for the decision to exclude. In the case of a non-United Kingdom citizen excluded from the United Kingdom, the notice is as shown on p.82.

The notice of exclusion informs the person to be excluded that it is an offence to fail to comply with the order and that she/he may make representations against it. It gives no explanation why the order has been made.

Solicitors are thus in the impossible position of hazarding guesses at the police evidence and attempting to refute unknown allegations in making representations to the Home Secretary. They are in no position to explore the evidence with their client or to pursue any line of enquiry not supplied by the client. Furthermore, they have no legal right to be present at the interview with the Adviser.

The existence of the Adviser is an attempt to disguise the unfettered nature of the power given to the Home Secretary and in no way represents an impartial assessment of the case.

Lord Alport, one of the two original Advisers, did not first look at the police evidence before he interviewed the suspect. Indeed he made a virtue of this decision by saying it might lead him inadvertently to ask awkward questions, whereas the opposite is in fact the case: if he were aware of the evidence he could ensure that he avoided incriminating questions; ignorant of the evidence he might inadvertently do so. The following is taken from the transcripts of an interview:

'My name is Alport. I am one of the advisers appointed by the Home Secretary to give him advice as to whether an exclusion order should be maintained or revoked. This is not a court of law. This is not an interrogation by me. The object is to try and add to the background of the grounds for the representations that you have made against the exclusion order, so that I may be able to judge fairly to the best of my ability as to what advice I give to the Secretary of State. I have not seen the police evidence. I have not done so for two reasons. One is that I wanted to meet you and ask you certain questions in order to get from you certain information which may be helpful to me in making my decision. I do not want to be prejudiced in any way at this particular moment at our interview by having read a record of whatever allegations are made against you by the police. That is the first reason.

'The second reason is that I do not want to be placed in a position whereby I might ask you questions which might be of an incriminating nature. Therefore I come to meet you on this occasion having before me only two documents'. (A letter from the excluded person and another from his solicitor).

It is particularly disturbing that the Advisers do not need any particular legal experience or any knowledge of Northern Ireland or of political groups operating in Britain. If the police evidence is not discussed, the interview can do no more than provide the Adviser with a general impression of the suspect's credibility. This may hinge on his/or her involvement with perfectly legal political groups of which the Adviser may disapprove – he may for instance be more inclined to recommend exclusion for a supporter of a united Ireland than for a person advocating continuing direct rule. The standard of advice rests solely upon the Adviser, for he can adopt any procedure for the interview he thinks fit.

Aware of a police dossier of allegedly incriminating evidence (which the suspect has not seen and cannot rebut), the Adviser might be expected at the very least to inform himself of the political views of the potential excludee. What group does he belong to? Does it support military action? What is its attitude to the political use of violence? And so on. The following quotation is taken from a transcript of an interview which took place after four members of Clann na h'Eireann had already been excluded on Lord Alport's advice.

(The suspect has just said that he is a member of Sinn Fein in Britain).

Alport: This is completely different from Cann na h'Eirinn? *(sic)*.

Answer: Completely.

Alport: Is this the Provisional?

Answer: Yes, Sinn Fein.

Alport: The Provisional side of it?

Answer: This is right.

Alport: Cann na h'Eirinn *(sic)* is the political wing of the Official IRA, is that correct?

Answer: That is correct.

Alport: This is the political wing of the Provisional IRA?

Answer: Yes.

Excluded persons

Former Home Secretary Roy Jenkins claimed to have rid Britain of 'dangerous terrorists' – 'the most experienced leaders of the Official and Provisional IRA'. One would expect that the main interest of the Government in such cases would be to prosecute these dangerous and experienced individuals for any past offences, and to prevent them from committing any others. This can hardly be achieved by alerting them to the police's interest in their activities, and removing them from one part of the country only to allow them to move freely in another. In fact the official justification for exclusions fails to stand up to scrutiny either way. If excludees are indeed 'dangerous criminals', the people of Northern Ireland are right to complain that their territory is being used as a 'dumping ground'. If they are not, the fact of their exclusion is a glaring act of injustice.

Of the 48 people excluded during 1979, one was a young man who had only just arrived in Britain – having come here with the help of the Royal Ulster Constabulary itself. **'John Smith'** had been arrested and convicted in Belfast, while a teenager, on charges of IRA membership and involvement in a hijack and arson. During his prison sentence, the Provisional IRA came to believe that he had given information to the security services. Knowing that his life would be in danger after he was released from prison, he sought the help of the Peace People who, with the RUC's assistance, arranged for him to come to Britain. He was released from prison in November 1979. It was accepted during the trial that he was, at most, a reluctant member of the Provisional IRA and his probation officer and the Peace People believed he was determined to get away from Belfast and start a new life. Shortly after his release from prison, he came to Britain and went to the home of the family which had agreed to put him up while he looked for a job. The following day, he was arrested by the police and held for seven days. He was served with an exclusion order and returned to Belfast. Representations made by his solicitor and probation officer were unsuccessful.

In February 1978, **John McKenna** was excluded. He had come to live in Britain five years earlier and had married an English woman. They settled in Kent and had two children. He was arrested under the Act, detained for questioning, transferred to Brixton prison and served with an exclusion order. His representations were rejected and he was flown to Belfast. Like other excluded persons, he was not re-arrested on arrival and he returned to the Falls, to the Catholic estate in Belfast where he had grown up. His English wife – who is not a Catholic – and their two daughters decided they had no choice but to follow him, even though his wife had little prospect of settling down and neither had any prospect of getting a job. The Kent solicitor who made representations on his behalf objected strongly to the whole proceedings:

> The Act however works extremely harshly and no doubt unfairly in cases such as Mr McKenna where there must be a real doubt as to whether or not he was really involved in any terrorist activities in Northern Ireland or in England which would have justified his exclusion from England . . . One of my main concerns with this case is the fact that Mr McKenna's wife is English and the two children of the marriage were born in England whereas the making of the exclusion order virtually forced her and the children to leave their country of origin.

The solicitor also pointed out that, since the suspect faced with an exclusion order is never charged with a criminal offence, no legal aid is available other than the extremely limited 'Green Form' scheme. The excludee therefore either has to find private funds or depend on the willingness of a solicitor to take on the case without payment.

On 12 December 1979, the police raided a large number of homes in London, Southampton, Birmingham and Liverpool. Amongst those detained in Southampton were **James Martin,** his wife and two of their children. A third child was away at the time. Although Veronica Martin and the children were released after 11 hours, James was detained for seven days until he was excluded. After reaching Northern Ireland, he made unsuccessful representations. James had lived in this country for 19 years – only one year short of the time-limit (under the 1976 Act) for exemption from exclusion. All three children were born in Britain. The Martin family decided they had no option but to go to Belfast. The Northern Ireland Housing Executive refused to house them and Veronica was unable to obtain financial assistance with the costs of removing their furniture from their council house in Southampton.

In one case known to NCCL, a man and a woman then engaged, now married, were *both* excluded – but *not* to the same part of the United Kingdom. John McLoughlin, then a 23-year-old glazier, used to visit Northern Ireland from his home in Glasgow, initially with a football team and later to see his girlfriend. She had once been convicted of a scheduled* offence and had subsequently been excluded from Great Britain. In July 1981 he was excluded from Northern Ireland and they were therefore prevented from being in any part of the United Kingdom together. They now live in the Republic of Ireland with their young child and cannot go as a family to visit her grandparents. When the Secretary of State reviewed Mr McLoughlin's case he gave no reasons for his continued exclusion. Mr McLoughlin is a British citizen and insists that his visits to Northern Ireland were personal and non-political. In his own words he has been 'forced like a refugee to seek refuge and scrounge for my upkeep in a foreign country'.

In many cases, the exclusion of the only or main breadwinner forces the family to choose between going to Northern Ireland or remaining in poverty in Britain. The family may have left Northern Ireland in the first place to escape the troubles; the wife and children may in fact be English and understandably unwilling to move to a strange place, devastated by a decade of violence. The problems are even greater if the marriage is 'mixed'. As former MP Gerry Fitt said about a number of his constituents during the debate on the 1976 Bill:

'The men involved are Belfast men married to English wives, and their children are English born. The men have been in

---

* An offence listed in the schedule to the Emergency Provisions Act 1978 and hence covered by its provisions.

steady jobs while they have lived in Southampton. Their children go to English schools and speak with English accents. They are unsuited to be sent back to Northern Ireland to live in areas where an English accent might get them into trouble. I have spoken to these people and I am convinced that they are not and never have been involved in terrorist activities in this island.'

If a wage-earner is imprisoned following conviction in the courts, the families are helped by the state with the cost of travel to the prisons. Exclusion denies them such help. Although Lord Shackleton suggested that families should be given financial aid to help with visiting, the Home Secretary said in the March 1980 renewal debate: 'I have considered the possibility of providing assistance towards the removal expenses of such families, but I have come to the conclusion that such a scheme would not be justified.'

The power of exclusion affects not only those against whom an order is made: NCCL has received disturbing reports from people who allege that, having travelled from Ireland or Northern Ireland to Britain, they have been ordered by the police to return home. With the threat of detention and permanent exclusion hanging over them, such people do not normally protest: but the 'exclusion' never appears in the official record.

In October 1980, NCCL was contacted by a probation officer at Maidstone prison. One of her clients, who had been convicted of conspiracy to cause explosions, had been granted parole on the advice of the Parole Board. The day before he was due to be released, he was informed by the governor that he would be detained for a further 15 days while the Home Secretary decided whether or not to exclude him. The Parole Board must have taken into account the nature of this man's offence before deciding to recommend him for parole. They were impressed by the fact that he had a home and a job to return to, and presumably believed that he was not likely to become involved in crime again. It therefore seems extraordinary that the Home Secretary should consider overruling the Parole Board's decision in this fashion.

In April 1981 the Act was used to exclude someone who had just been *acquitted* of criminal charges.

Robert Storey was a co-defendant in the trial which followed an attempt to spring from Brixton prison Brian Keenan, who was then on remand on a charge of conspiracy to cause explosions (for which he was later convicted). The jury failed to agree a verdict in Storey's first trial for conspiracy to effect Keenan's escape and for possession of firearms; on the re-trial he was acquitted. Immediately Storey was released from custody he was re-arrested under the Prevention of Terrorism Act and excluded.

Early in 1985 a man was released from Hull Prison after serving a ten-year sentence. A family friend travelled from Birmingham to arrive at the prison at 7 a.m. to meet him, only to find that he had been released at 4 a.m. – into police custody. An exclusion order had been served on him and he was removed to the Republic that night. No-one had informed his family that this would happen.

Although practical campaigning is clearly preferable to violence, the Government has hardly been welcoming towards Sinn Fein members elected through the ballot box to the Northern Ireland Assembly and in 1985 in the local elections there. When two Sinn Fein Assembly members **Gerry Adams** and **Danny Morrison** were invited to London in 1982 by a group of Labour GLC Councillors, the Home Secretary William Whitelaw invoked the Act to exclude them. Both were banned from entering Great Britain, together with a third Assembly member, Martin McGuiness. Whitelaw had in fact met Adams secretly ten weeks previously, when Whitelaw was Northern Ireland Secretary and before Adams had been elected to any position by Northern Ireland voters. Ken Livingstone, GLC leader, later visited Belfast to meet the Sinn Fein leaders. As Liz Curtis writes in her book *Ireland: the Propaganda War:* '. . . the exclusion of Adams and Morrison the previous December had highlighted the desire of many politicians and editors to banish the whole discomforting issue to the other side of the Irish Sea, and to deny any contact, whether through personal meetings or the transmission of ideas, between republicans and people in Britain.'

Press outrage at the prospect of prominent Sinn Feiners visiting London was widespread, although it was nowhere suggested that they would be planning crimes of a terrorist nature during their visit.

Against exclusion orders

The Government argues that its job is to prevent acts of terrorism as well as to ensure that criminals are punished. It is therefore necessary to anticipate events, and to take action even in circumstances where the available evidence would not secure a conviction. Court action would be preferable but, they argue, the type of evidence gathered by police against excluded people is 'too sensitive', related to 'national security' or would not otherwise stand up in court. Lord Shackleton termed it 'highly classified'.

'Sensitive information' often comes from paid informers or other unnamed sources, who remain unidentified and cannot therefore be called to court as witnesses. National security would cover almost any matter relating to the strategy and tactics of the police in dealing with terrorist-type offences. According to the Jellicoe report, applications for exclusion orders are filtered through the National Joint Unit at Scotland Yard by the police force in whose area the subject is found. The application is forwarded to the Home Office, where it is considered by various officials, the Minister, and finally the Secretary of State who must sign it.

Lord Jellicoe noted, in a remarkable understatement, that the submission prepared by Home Office officials, based on the police report, 'is generally more substantial than that for an extension of detention, because it is recognised that an exclusion order has a more fundamental and usually a harsher, effect on its subject than the extension by five days of his period in police custody'.

The introduction of exclusion orders has given the United Kingdom its own system of 'internal exile'. Lord Jellicoe described it as 'the most extreme of the Act's powers: in its effects on civil liberties, it is in my view more severe than any other power in the Act; in its procedure and principles it departs more thoroughly from the normal criminal process (and) it has aroused substantial resentment even among many, particularly in Northern Ireland, who support the aims and content of the remainder of the legislation.' Yet he accepted the arguments of the Government and its officials that 'there have undoubtedly been cases where exclusion has rid Great Britain of dangerous terrorists'.

The Government argued, in support of the re-enactment of these powers in the 1984 Act, that exclusion is not a punishment. But exclusion involves compulsory removal to another part of the country; separation from friends and, often, family; a prohibition on return; and, for those returned to Northern Ireland, a risk of injury or death in the violence there.

Lord Jellicoe considered whether the decision to exclude a person should be that of a court or tribunal rather than the Secretary of State. He concluded that it could not because: 'Exclusion is a matter of public policy. It is based not merely on the conduct of the excluded person, but also, once his terrorist involvement is established – on matters such as the security situation at the time . . .' He refused to accept that such a decision, depriving an individual of his or her liberty, *should* be capable of judicial assessment or should not be made. It is unacceptable precisely because it is a punishment imposed by the executive without recourse to the Courts.

Lord Jellicoe considered that the Minister's accountability to Parliament is sufficient to ensure that the powers are used properly. But the Minister never discusses such cases in Parliament. MPs cannot see the police evidence and may not even know the decision has been made. They certainly cannot question it.

There can be no accountability to Parliament for individual case decisions at all.

Lord Shackleton found that the value of the information in the police dossier depended on 'careful gradings and assessment'. The dossier contains information such as any criminal record, information about political activity as well as unsubstantiated statements obtained by the police, possibly after a suspect has been detained for several days under the Act.

Uncorroborated statements may also be obtained from informers whose motives must be suspect. There may be financial pressure or personal malice involved. There is no way of testing whether an informer in fact acted as an *agent provocateur,* who actively encouraged the person to engage in illegal activity. Statements may be supplied by someone eager to satisfy the police or by someone with a personal grudge against the suspect or from people also held under the Act itself.

Silence during the interrogation may also encourage the police to apply for an exclusion order. Lord Shackleton stated in his report:

> The police often find that the person concerned will say nothing to them at all. They realise that there can be several reasons for this and indeed the person concerned is not bound to say anything. But the police cannot rule out the possibility that he has been trained in what might be called 'anti-interrogation' techniques and that this may be an indication of involvement in a terrorist organisation.

As long as the suspect and his or her lawyer are refused the right to know the accusations made against him or her, the right to challenge the evidence and cross-examine prosecution witnesses, and the right to a judicial hearing and appeal, there must be an overwhelming probability that people are excluded on the basis of inaccurate evidence. But an exclusion order can be as damning as a criminal conviction.

Legal advice obtained by the NCCL indicates that it is not possible to challenge an exclusion order successfully in the UK courts. The Act gives the Secretary of State the power to exclude anyone provided he is 'satisfied' that the excludee is involved in terrorism. The Secretary of State's subjective judgement can only be challenged if the excluded person can show evidence that the decision was made in bad faith – an impossible task. The only way of establishing evidence of bad faith would be to commence a legal action and obtain all the documentation involved in the case – but such disclosure would be refused on the grounds that it would be damaging to 'the public interest'.

NCCL believes that the system of exclusion violates the European Convention on Human Rights, Article 6 of which provides that in the determination of their civil rights or in any criminal proceedings against them, everyone is entitled to a fair and public hearing within a reasonable time by an independent and impartial tribunal established by law. Furthermore, anyone charged with an offence has the right to be informed of the nature and cause of the accusation against them and to challenge witnesses. Article 14 of the Convention provides that implementation of Convention rights must be made without discrimination on grounds of religion or national origin. And Article 13 provides that anyone who believes that his Convention rights have been infringed shall have the right to a remedy within their own country. As we have seen, it is impossible to challenge an exclusion order successfully in the British courts, while *habeas corpus* has proved ineffective in Prevention of Terrorism Act cases.

The existence of the exclusion power has made it impossible for the United Kingdom to ratify Protocol Four of the Convention, which declares the right to freedom of movement within one's own country and the right to choose one's own residence.

In October 1980, NCCL initiated a complaint to the European Human Rights Commission on behalf of **Danny Ryan,** who was born in Ireland. He was living with his family in Bristol when he was arrested under the Prevention of Terrorism Act in January 1975 and served with an exclusion order. His representations were unsuccessful and he was removed to Dublin. As a result, he was separated from his five eldest children who stayed in England; his two younger children, who joined him in Dublin, were forced to interrupt their education, abandon their schools and leave the rest of their family. In July 1979, he applied to the Home Secretary for a review of the exclusion order which had by then been in force for over four years. The Home Secretary refused to revoke the order and Danny Ryan complained to the European Commission of the continuing infringement of his right to family life. Regrettably, the Commission declared the application inadmissible, arguing that the right to family life does not include non-dependant children or grandchildren.

Arrest and detention

What the Act says about arrest

Under Section 12 of the Act, *1984* a police constable can arrest a person without a warrant if he/she reasonably suspects:

(i) that he or she belongs to or supports a proscribed organisation and/or
(ii) that he or she is subject to an exclusion order or has helped or harboured any other person who is subject to an exclusion order and/or
(iii) that he or she has solicited, lent, given or received money or other property for use in connection with acts of terrorism and/or,
(iv) that he or she is concerned in the commission, preparation or instigation of any acts of terrorism (except acts connected solely with the affairs of the United Kingdom or any part of the UK other than Northern Ireland).

What the Act says about detention

Once a person has been arrested he or she can be held by the police for up to 48 hours and then for up to five more days on the authority of the Secretary of State. During this time a suspect need not be charged with an offence nor brought to court.

The requirement to obtain the Home Secretary's permission for a further five days' detention is, in the Government's view, an adequate safeguard. In England and Wales, the police submit a report via the National Joint Unit at Scotland Yard, in writing to the Home Office (or Scottish Office) whose officials advise the Minister of State and the Secretary of State, although where time is exceptionally short, a senior police officer may explain the background to the Secretary of State in person, or if necessary a Minister of State. Lord Shackleton revealed that where a Minister or Secretary of State is not available, authority is granted by a senior official in the Home Office until the Secretary of State can consider the case himself.

During the Commons Committee debates on the 1983 Bill the Home Office Minister, David Waddington, rejected a Labour proposal that each case should be reviewed by a magistrate after 36 hours (as under the Police and Criminal Evidence Act) on the grounds that 'in many cases information may not be disclosed publicly because to disclose it may imperil the lives of others'.

The Judges' Rules – the guidelines for treatment of people by the police – apply to arrests under the Act. These are being replaced in January 1986 by provisions in the Police and Criminal Evidence Act and its 'Codes of Practice for the Detention, Treatment, Questioning and Identification of Persons by the Police and for the Searching of Premises and Seizure of Property'.

In limited respects, the rights of those held under the PTA will, under the new Police and Criminal Evidence Act, be the same as those of other suspects. For example, they will have the right to be told the reason for their arrest. Once at the police station, the police officer in charge ('custody officer') will have to make a written record of the grounds for the detention and inform the suspect of the reason. The Police and Criminal Evidence Act specifically states that the person's unqualified right to have someone informed of their arrest applies to those arrested or detained under the PTA (Section 55 (10)). However, while 'ordinary' suspects must be given this right within 36 hours, those held under the PTA must have that right only within 48 hours. Similarly the right of 'ordinary' suspects to see a solicitor within 36 hours (if not before) is postponed to within 48 hours for PTA suspect. Moreoever, if a senior officer (Commander or Assistant Chief Constable) has reasonable grounds for believing that allowing a suspect held under the PTA to see a solicitor 'will lead to interference' in the gathering of information about acts of terrorism or, by alerting any person, make it more difficult to prevent such an act or apprehend the person responsible, he can insist that the suspect can only consult a solicitor 'in the sight and hearing' of a police officer unconnected with the case. (Section 57 (15))

After the arrest the police are allowed to take any 'reasonably necessary steps' for identification, including photographing, measuring and fingerprinting. This can be done without the suspect's consent or a court order. 'Reasonable force' can be used if the suspect does not co-operate. The 'safeguards' in the Police and Criminal and Evidence Act limiting the circumstances in which the police may take a suspect's fingerprints do not apply to those held under the PTA, nor those relating to the destruction of the fingerprints of those cleared of the offence (see p.41).

The Codes of Practice under the Police and Criminal Evidence Act will not have the force of law. But the Act does state that police officers who breach the code are liable to disciplinary proceedings. The code specifically indicates which 'rights' apply to those held under the PTA and how these rights are restricted. The code restates, for instance, the right to legal advice but only 'within 48 hours'. But the code relating to physical conditions of detention – heating, meals and lighting – is the same as for other suspects, as are those concerning medical treatment, e.g. that a police surgeon should be called to examine any suspect who alleges he or she has been assaulted in custody. Suspects should also be asked if they wish their own doctor to be called. If suspects want to be examined at any time the code says that they may be examined by a doctor of their choice.

In any 24-hour period the person detained must be allowed a continuous period of at least eight hours rest and when questioned should not be required to stand. Each interviewing officer should identify him or herself. No officer should use or threaten violence, or use inducements to obtain a statement.

Search of persons and premises

The PTA also gives the police the power to stop and search, without a warrant, anyone suspected of involvement in terrorism, in order to establish whether the suspect has any documents or articles on them which could show that they were liable for arrest.

A police officer who is searching premises with a search warrant is allowed under the Act to search every person found in the premises named in the warrant. An officer with the rank of superintendent or above can sign a note authorising a search, if he considers the case is one of great emergency and immediate action is necessary 'in the interest of the state' – thus removing the need to obtain a magistrate's approval.

Any officer using these powers of search, can seize anything which he has reasonable grounds for suspecting to be evidence of an offence relating to a proscribed organisation or an exclusion order. He can also take anything which he reasonably suspects is evidence which would be sufficient to justify the Home Secretary in banning an organisation or making an exclusion order.

Arrest at ports of entry

Under Section 13, the Secretary of State is authorised to confer on examining officers (police, immigration officers, some Customs and Excise officers and, in Northern Ireland, soldiers) powers of 'detention'. Under these powers, officers can 'examine' anyone entering Great Britain.

Unlike arrests inland under Section 12, the officials do not need to have any suspicion at all that the person is involved in terrorism, having the power to detain anyone to establish whether they are, (or whether they have breached an exclusion order or assisted someone else to do so). In a case in 1980, Lord Justice Donaldson confirmed that the officials need have *no suspicion* before they detain the 'suspect': 'an officer has to satisfy himself that the person whom he seeks to examine is in the category of person where he can say to himself bona fide "I wish to find out whether this person has, for example, information which he or she should have disclosed (about terrorism)". He does not have to have any grounds for thinking that they have the information.' (Divisional Court, 30 October 1980, unreported)

Lord Jellicoe argued that it would not be possible to require the officials to have 'reasonable suspicion' that the person was involved in terrorism (the requirement for an arrest inland) because 'it is only in rare cases that he will at this stage have formed more than *faint doubts* as to the passenger's bona fides' . . . 'Most of the time the decision to examine a passenger is based more on an examining officer's *instinct* and on experience than on specific intelligence.' (our emphasis)

Lord Jellicoe did however recommend that the officials be required to have 'reasonable suspicion' if they wanted to detain the suspect for more than twelve hours, a recommendation which was incorporated in the Supplemental Order to the Act. As in the case of Section 12 arrests, after 48 hours the authorisation of the Secretary of State is needed to detain the suspect for a further one to five days.

In recent years, about 45,000 individuals per year have been stopped at ports in England & Wales, questioned and searched and then released within one hour. (see Table 11, p.81).

The record in Great Britain

Between 29 November 1974 and 31 December 1984, 5905 people were arrested *in connection with Northern Ireland terrorism*, of whom 821 were held for more than 48 hours. Of those arrested, 4175 (71%) were held at ports of entry and 1730 (29%) elsewhere. 275 people were served with exclusion orders, 152 were charged with offences under the Act, 13 with conspiracy to commit offences under the Act and 294 with other offences.

Of these 5905 people arrested and detained during the ten years operation of the Acts, the vast majority – 87.5% (5,171) were neither excluded nor charged with a criminal offence. In all only 459 people – 7.7% of those detained – were charged with any criminal offence (including offences under the PTA and those returned to Northern Ireland and charged). Many of the offences involved were extremely serious – including murder, firearms and explosives offences. But many concerned theft or similar offences not involving violence. Of the 152 people detained and charged under the Act itself, charges were dropped in fifteen cases and 21 people were acquitted. One was awaiting trial and 115 people were found guilty. Of the 307 charged with other offences, charges were dropped in 32 cases and 30 were acquitted. Eighteen people were still awaiting trial when the statistics were published. Of the 227 people convicted, 94 received non-custodial sentences (a fine or an absolute or conditional discharge); 31 were imprisoned for twelve months or less; 34 for between one and five years; and 63 for five years or more. Five were sentenced to borstal or a detention centre. (NB The figure of 307 charged with other offences, in Table 7 of the Home Office statistics, is at slight variance with its earlier figure of 294 in Table 1 quoted above).

During the first nine months of the operation of the 1984 Act (April to December 1984), 44 people were detained *in connection with international terrorism*. The majority (39) were inland arrests. In 16 of these cases, the Secretary of State granted an extension of detention, beyond 48 hours. Five people were detained at a port or airport; of whom two were held more than 48 hours. Eight people were charged with 'an offence'. 23 people were neither charged with any offence nor deported. Thirteen of those detained in connection with international terrorism were subsequently deported under the Immigration Act 1971.

The vast majority of all the arrests under the PTA took place in Liverpool (1364, 23%), London (1280, 21%) and Dumfries and Galloway (1222, 20%).

Of the 158 persons detained but not charged or excluded during 1984, 139 were held for less than 48 hours, one for two to three days, four for three to four days, five for four to six days and nine for six to seven days.

During the 1979 General Election, Labour Party canvassers in the London constituency of Hampstead were arrested under the Act. **Margaret Fletcher,** a student at Middlesex Polytechnic, and **Nick Mullen,** another student and a member of the Troops Out Movement, were arrested on polling day while 'knocking up' voters. Ms Fletcher was strip-searched and released after a period in the cells, but Mr Mullen was held for a longer period of questioning. It appeared that the officers who arrested them had been watching a flat owned by Paddy Prendeville, a journalist with *Hibernia* magazine in Dublin. As we describe below, Paddy Prendeville was himself arrested under the Act in December 1979.

Many of those detained under the Act are students or political activists travelling between Ireland or Northern Ireland and Britain for conferences. In December 1977, seven delegates to the National Union of Students annual conference were arrested at Blackpool airport, one being held overnight on the grounds of an alleged association with the Provisional IRA. All were released without charge. In June 1978, a Student Community Action worker from Nottingham University was taking a party of young people on a holiday to Nottingham, from Belfast: two of the 16-year-old Catholic boys in the group were arrested, detained for three hours, searched, photographed and fingerprinted. In November of the same year, two students in a party of students and trades unionists visiting Britain for the 'Peace, Jobs, Progress' campaign were detained at the airports in Belfast and Manchester. Like the boys in Nottingham, they complained of police abuse during their period of detention.

In February 1979, **Helen Connor,** then a vice-president of the NUS, was stopped by Special Branch officers at Belfast airport while on union business, and detained for three hours. On her return she was held for a further two hours at Heathrow. She complained that in addition to being searched and fingerprinted by male officers, her documents were photocopied. In December 1979, two members of the Northern Ireland delegation to the NUS conference were detained at Liverpool airport. One of them, **Patricia Clarke,** complained that she was subject to a full body search in front of six male police officers.

In October 1980, **Margaret McNulty,** a delegate from the Republican Clubs (a lawful Republican organisation in Northern Ireland), was arrested at Heathrow airport on her way to a feminist conference in London. Two other women travelling to the same conference were also arrested and detained.

Others have been held when passing through the UK. On 29 October 1979 two men who were in transit to Holland to work were arrested at Heathrow airport and detained for six days. **Hugh Leekey,** who was arrested on 15 November 1979, had arrived in Liverpool that morning and was due to sign a contract of work with the Ocean Fleet Line for an eight month period. He was detained for 24 hours, although he claims he was only questioned for 30 minutes. He lost the job and had to return to Belfast.

The powers given to examining officers at ports of entry encourage fishing operations designed to collect information or simply to intimidate political activists. The case of **Margaretta D'Arcy,** a well-known socialist playwright, is not unusual. She was held on 9 January 1980 and describes her experience thus:

> I was travelling from Belfast to London and on leaving the boat at Stranraer (approx 5.30 pm) I had my luggage searched.

Inside my bag were a number of pamphlets about the conditions of the H-block prisoners in Northern Ireland. I was brought to the police station, having been taken to a police office in the dockside railway station. I had already filled in the regular form giving my name, address, journey particulars and business. I was told in the railway police office that I was being arrested under the PTA. At the town police station I refused to answer any questions; stating that this was a violation of the Human Rights Charter to which both Britain and Ireland were signatories. Present were two police officers (one 'nice' and one 'nasty') and a woman 'search-officer'. The 'nasty' one tried to rile me with sexual innuendoes about 'Sabrina's Bra', in reference to women's lib. I pointed out that sexual humiliations were expressly mentioned in the Bennett Report as an improper activity for the police, and he shut up. I had on me copies of the Human Rights Charter, the Amnesty Report and the Bennett Report. If I had not had this documentation, I am sure the 'nasty' policeman would have gone much further in psychological harassment. No more questions were asked of me, and I was let go after an hour and a half. I knew no-one in Stranraer and accordingly felt very vulnerable. The entire procedure seemed to have no purpose other than to instill fear into me.

Arriving at Holyhead to board the ferry in April 1983, authoress **Dervla Murphy** found herself detained for 20 minutes for a 'security check' under the PTA, the only passenger to be thus delayed. The officer searched her luggage and read her personal letters and bank statements. Puzzled at her detention, she discussed it later with a fellow passenger on the ferry who told her: 'You're wearing three anti-nuclear badges. I've learnt to take mine off, just to save time, when passing these security checks.'

Eamonn McCann, political correspondent for the Irish paper *The Sunday World,* was detained at Liverpool airport in July 1983. He had just completed a short speaking tour on the Fenian and Marxist movements of the 19th and early 20th century. He was held for eight hours during which time his requests to see a solicitor met only evasive answers. He was told that the number of his employer could not be reached, although he subsequently found that the newspaper's switchboard had been open during the entire time he was detained. Mr McCann was photographed, fingerprinted and asked for details of the meetings at which he had spoken, the organisers and participants.

Section 62 of the Criminal Law Act (entitling an arrested person to have someone informed of his/or her arrest and whereabouts) applies, in theory, to arrests under the Act (until the Police and Criminal Evidence Act comes into force in January 1986). But an exception permitting the police to refuse if delay 'is necessary in the interests of the police investigation, the prevention of crime or the apprehension of offenders' has ensured that a large number of people arrested under the PTA are held completely *incommunicado.*

Three Irishmen, **Jo Arbuckle, Eugene Barren and Aidan Lofgray,** who worked in Barnsley, went back to Northern Ireland to attend a friend's wedding in May 1980. On their return they were detained by the Liverpool police. No-one was informed. After two days, their Barnsley landlords, concerned at their delay without hearing from them, contacted their families in Northern Ireland.

A Liverpool solicitor agreed to look into the case on their behalf. The police admitted that three men were held, but refused to confirm their identities. Two of the three were subsequently served with exclusion orders (without access to any independent legal advice) and returned to Northern Ireland without making representations. The third was released. No-one was informed of the arrests and no access was given to the solicitor engaged by the men's families.

A further case illustrates that children may be innocent sufferers following a PTA arrest.

In March 1980 **Joe O'Brien** and **Michael Forgione,** together with Joe's eight-year-old daughter, Elizabeth, were arrested at Liverpool after driving from Northern Ireland across on the ferry to Leyland in Lancashire to collect some of Michael's furniture. On their return, they were arrested on the boat by the Liverpool police, only 15 minutes before the boat was due to leave.

Both men objected about the child and the police informed them that Elizabeth would be sent home by herself. The shipping company refused to take responsibility for her and her father refused to let her go on her own. By this time, Elizabeth was in hysterics at having been separated from her father. She asked to be sent to her aunt's home only a short distance away, but was sent instead to the Royal Liverpool Children's Hospital. Her aunt was not informed until 1.30 pm the following day – half an hour before the two men were freed.

No-one in Belfast was informed of the arrests. Joe's wife had gone to the police station to report them missing and only then was she told that there had been an emergency on board the boat and her child was in hospital. She was not unnaturally distraught, having no further information. When the child and father were reunited they were told to find their own way to the boat.

It is extremely difficult for a detainee to challenge the lawfulness of their arrest and detention by means of an action for false imprisonment. Examining officers at ports of entry – where nearly three-quarters of the arrests take place – are entitled to arrest someone solely on the basis of 'suspicion' of involvement in terrorism. There is no requirement of 'reasonable suspicion' which implies an objective test of the evidence and no court is likely to over-rule the officer's judgement. Inland, however, the arrest must be made on the normal basis of 'reasonable suspicion'. Nonetheless, arrests under the Act have rarely been successfully challenged.

Michael Connolly, a man with no previous criminal record and little interest in politics, succeeded in obtaining a court order for the destruction of his fingerprints and the record of his arrest under the Act. On 11 October 1977, he and two friends, a West German and an Australian, visited the Old Bailey, having heard on the news that the appeal of the IRA pub bombers was to be heard there.

Because of the IRA court case, special security checks were in operation including body searches at the entrance to the building. The Special Branch had set up an identity check at the entrance to the court, but on the understanding that members of the public who did not want to give their names and addresses should be able to enter any other court. Michael Connolly had no identification with him and knew that his name might cause him difficulties – although he is not Irish. He told his friends he would visit another court and meet them later. The Special Branch officers became suspicious at his disappearance and arrested his friends for refusing to supply his name. Michael Connolly, who was found sitting peacefully in another courtroom, was also arrested even after he had given his name and address. All three were then taken to Snow Hill police station.

Although Michael Connolly had now given his name and address and offered his landlady's name as a source of proof, he was photographed and had swabs taken to check for explosives. He was placed in a cell and told that he could be held for seven days. Uncertain about why he was being held at all, Michael Connolly objected to having his fingerprints taken and asked whether they would be returned or destroyed. He says that he was told he could write to the Police Commissioner, and then gave permission for his prints to be taken. While he was held, his flat was searched by police officers accompanied by dogs. He was released after 7½ hours' detention without, as counsel for the police later suggested, 'a stain on his character' – except for a newly-opened Special Branch file.

NCCL's legal officer represented Michael Connolly in his action for wrongful arrest and an application for an order that the documents, including fingerprints and photograph, be destroyed. The action was successful. The jury decided that because he had not been properly informed of the reasons for his arrest, the arrest was unlawful, and he was awarded nominal damages. More importantly, the judge ordered the destruction of the documents – an order against which the police did not appeal. But Michael Connolly was ordered to pay £180 in legal aid contribution.

Despite the finding in the Connolly case, the police have subsequently refused all claims by other people held under the Act for the destruction or return of the records. Before the case came to court, the then Minister of State, Lord Harris, had told Christopher Price MP that:

> The general principle is that while the powers contained in this Act remain in force, photographs and fingerprints of all persons detained are being retained centrally by the police. Details of persons detained are also kept for record purposes. I am afraid that, as with any such case, I can give no such assurance that Mr Connolly will not be questioned again in the future.

Although documents relating to Michael Connolly's detention have now been destroyed, anyone else who has once been held under the Act runs the risk of being arrested and detained again simply because the police or examining officers are aware of the earlier incident.

Michael Connolly is by no means the only person to be arrested simply because he was near a law court at the wrong time. In September 1975, 'Betty Jones', an Irish girl living and working in London, was showing her two sisters from Belfast around London. They parked their car, which had Northern Ireland registration plates, in the NCP car park near St Paul's Cathedral, which they planned to visit. They were quite unaware that the Guildford bombing trial had recently started in the Old Bailey nearby. They returned to find the car the object of a bomb scare. They willingly identified themselves to the police and accompanied the officers to Snow Hill police station to have their identification checked.

All three girls were detained for six days. They claim that their repeated requests to telephone their parents in Belfast were refused. One sister was woken early in the morning and asked to sign her name at the bottom of a blank statement sheet – 'just to provide a sample of your handwriting'! Their parents eventually contacted a Belfast solicitor who in turn alerted a London solicitor. He was allowed to see them the day before they were released. He explained that they were entitled to have food sent in (one of the girls, a vegetarian, had been unable to get suitable food). None of the girls was questioned during their period of detention.

Paddy Prendeville, then assistant editor of the Dublin magazine *Hibernia,* gave a vivid account of his arrest and detention at the end of a holiday in London in December 1979.

I never had a gun pointed at me before. But now there were three of them aimed straight at my heart held by three police officers shouting 'Don't move . . . turn around . . . hands against the wall'. As they searched and handcuffed me I noticed that their hands were gloved in polythene material, presumably to avoid fingerprinting the flat. One of them flexed his fingers and clenched his fists menacingly and his strange gloves only added to the threatening expression on his face as he warned me to stop talking to my companion.

Seconds earlier my friend and I had been squeezing the last few drops out of a whisky bottle. It was 4.15 am, Wednesday, 12 December, and the last night of what had been a very enjoyable holiday. The two thunderous bangs on the door (it had been broken down) were followed by the thumping of running feet in the hallway, and three pistol-toting men (one in uniform) burst through the living-room door followed by several others.

After the initial mayhem had died down, Detective Inspector Beck announced himself and told us that we were being arrested under the PTA. My protesting friend was told by the only woman police officer present that she would be strip-searched in front of the male officers if she did not shut up. They started to pull her pullover off and then led her into the kitchen.

On the way to Leman Street Police Station my escort – who I later discovered had the unlikely name of my childhood football hero, Bobby Charlton – joked with the others as we passed the Old Bailey. 'Want to nip in for a quick plea?' said one; 'It'll be all over in a few seconds', said another. They sniggered, as I protested my innocence with as much dignity as I could muster. Bobby Charlton then asked me how long I had been staying in the flat. When I told him I would answer no questions until I have seen my solicitor he came out with the first of several TV cop clichés that I was to hear over the next few days: 'Just remember sonny boy, it's very easy to slip and fall when you get out of this van'. Very reassuring!

Charlton's conversation and my own peace of mind did not improve in the next few hours as he swabbed my hands for traces of explosives (!) and took fingerprints, photos and other details from me. Ridiculing my protestations of innocence of any crime he gravely informed me that in his experience as a policeman 'dealing with the flotsam of society I never believe your kind'.

He asked me if I had any political views and I replied

cautiously that I supported the Irish dimension as enunciated by the Taoiseach, Charlie Haughey. This confused him thoroughly. 'Eh? What's a teeshuck? Who's this bloke Awee? Is he head of the IRA then?' He asked me if I had ever been in trouble before and refused to accept my negative reply, saying 'come on, you must have a record, you're Irish'.

The real interrogators were less racialist and definitely less amusing as I was soon to discover. I spent the first 24 hours in a filthy cell, completely naked for the first few hours as all my clothes had been taken off me, but was subjected to no questioning at all. My gloom and self-pity were not relieved by snatches of conversation from the next cell. A Mr Duffy asked why he had been arrested and was told that he was being held under the Prevention of Terrorism Act to which he retorted: 'I'm 67 years of age, how in the name of Jesus could I terrorise anybody?' The conversation ended abruptly with the clanking of cell door, lock and key.

But on the Thursday morning I was led upstairs to an office by two well-dressed members of the Anti-Terrorist Squad (ATS) who proceeded, with chilling efficiency, to administer to me the most terrifying few days of my life. After cursory details of my life and family had been taken they insisted that I had no right to silence.

They dismissed the solicitors I mentioned as hack lawyers who were only interested in money. I was also told that the least I could expect was to be charged under Section 11 of the PTA. I eventually agreed to give details of my movements, starting with the Thursday afternoon when I had landed at London's Heathrow Airport, and so I described in detail the first few hours of my visit. This concluded the third two-hour session of the day and I was led down to my cell.

But that night I thought over my position again. I realised that even my innocent 'alibi', which would include references to dozens of individuals and friends I had met in the last few days, most of them concerned in left-wing politics, could inadvertently place question marks over others and even myself. I determined, whatever the consequences, to answer no more questions.

On the Friday morning they became very threatening and interrogator number one told me that I was definitely linked to the 'hair-raising' events of the last few days which he claimed were even bigger than the exploits of the Balcombe Street IRA unit. 'It would make your hair curl, Paddy', he kept repeating. His number two nodded seriously in agreement. Number one then threw a second bombshell at me: 'We also have evidence to link you with Airey Neave's murder last March!'

I could feel my jaw sag as he started to question me about various political activities in Ireland. The fact that I knew some of those named (as indeed my job requires) appeared to be proof positive in his mind that I was implicated in the two most serious offences of 1979. But more was to come. He leaned over the table into my face and said, 'I told you that you are linked to the two biggest terrorist crimes of the last twelve months; well, I was wrong, you're also involved in a third – the Provo bombs in London last Christmas!' I nearly fainted and he walked over to the door. 'Let's bring him down to his cell', he said to number two, 'and I hope your hair does not turn white tonight, Paddy, I bet you don't get much sleep', he added.

He was correct about the lack of sleep. It was now the third night, and since Thursday morning I had been subjected to six sessions of interrogation, each lasting two hours. My feeling of isolation and despair was complete. I remembered a remark by number one about juries being very impressionable. He was warning me that twelve good English men and true would be very impressed by the weight of such allegations no matter how circumstantial or spurious the evidence. I decided to shut up altogether, not only about my visit to London but everything and anything.

The next morning, Saturday, I tried to appear determined as I announced my intention to remain completely silent. I told them that they had terrified me (which was true) by accusing me of several major crimes. As each innocuous answer I had given only seemed to incriminate me, I was saying nothing until I saw my solicitor.

Number one looked quite angry and repeated that I was in it up to my neck. 'A right hornets' nest', he added, 'but I'll tell you what I'll do. If you tell us exactly what we want to know' (he paused and I waited for the offer of a Queen's pardon for offences which I had not committed) 'at end of the day I'll see you fine'. Assuring myself that I would not have accepted any offer (no informer me, not even of fiction!) never mind his ridiculous one, I repeated my adamant intention to remain silent.

They suddenly became very concerned. How could they persuade me that they only wanted to help me? I answered, again truthfully, that they could not. Then suddenly they changed course. They assured me that their main concern was to prove my innocence which they were almost convinced of. They had not really accused me of involvement in the incidents mentioned. The number two (a Scot) assured me that he actually had many Irish friends; they were great people, 'nice and decent just like you Paddy'. I smiled for the first time in four days and number one raised his eyes to the ceiling. He leaned over and told me to seize my self-confidence. 'You're a man, aren't you Paddy. I suppose you would prefer us to beat you; then you could hate us and it would cause no problems resisting us'.

I was not at all sure about this but decided to agree with him, adding the black lie that I thought they were very civilised. 'Well then', he said, 'why not be straight with us'. I tried to look non-committal and number one asked me if I would like some lunch. My stomach heaved at the thought of any food, but anything was better than this game of poker and so I tried to look as if no more appetising suggestion had ever been made to me and we adjourned.

They were back in a couple of hours with more sweetness and kindness. Would I like a change of clothes that my sister had brought in? There was a toothbrush and paste in the same bag. Would I like to use them? They didn't mention that my sister's parcel was handed in 48 hours earlier. With a whimper of gratitude I accepted the offers and spent about five minutes furiously brushing my teeth for the first time in four days.

Sitting down to our next session I was swamped with kindly offers of coffee, fruit that my sister had sent in ('little angel isn't she', said one) and, absolute luxury, clean underwear. I accepted all the blandishments as gracefully as possible and waited for their next move.

It came in the form of a political diatribe against IRA extremism and an appeal to my moderate sensibilities. I still insisted on remaining silent and there was another long pause. 'O.K!' sighed one, 'bring him down to his cell'.

Ten minutes later they returned to the cell and casually asked me if I would like to go. As calmly as possible I walked to the cell door and, after collecting some personal items at the station sergeant's desk, I was ushered to the two ATS members' car. I declined their offer of a pint (had they discovered the best way to make me talk?) and we arrived at my sister's house at approximately 6 p.m.

My sister shot them a venomous glance and with a cheerio they walked into the Kilburn evening.

In some cases, extended detention produces a severe psychological reaction. **Bernard Martin** was arrested in Southampton on 12 December 1979 and detained until the 16th, when he was taken to hospital. He discharged himself two days later, and was seen the following day by a psychiatrist. According to the account which Bernard Martin gave to the doctor, his house was raided by police and he was arrested at about 4 a.m. He was taken to the police station, questioned briefly and placed in a cell. From then on he began to experience a series of 'bizarre and disturbing' hallucinations. Martin's doctor said that he had no major previous medical problems and no history of psychiatric disturbance requiring treatment; nor is there any record of his having received psychiatric treatment in Southampton previously. Medical examination showed bruising on the margin of the right eye, one shoulder, and the upper arm. The psychiatrist concluded that Martin had suffered 'from an abnormal mental state of a psychotic kind' and that his symptoms 'are those which it is known can occur when people are kept in conditions of isolation or sensory deprivation. If a person is placed in an unfamiliar setting without his normal social supports and environmental surroundings with irregular meals and artificial light, this clinical picture can result. The anxiety of being kept in police custody is an important additional factor.'

Like many others who fear repeated arrest or harassment, Mr Martin decided not to make a complaint or take legal action.

Against the arrest and detention powers

These extensive powers of arrest, detention and search have been defended on the grounds that they result in convictions which would otherwise not be obtained and that they enable the police to gather information about terrorist activity. Neither of these arguments is legitimate. The extended powers cannot be justified by the need to bring suspects before the courts on criminal charges because the police already had wide powers to arrest anyone suspected of involvement in terrorist activity.

All the people detained under the Act and subsequently charged with criminal offences could have been arrested and questioned without using the detention powers of the Act itself. Roy Jenkins, as Home Secretary, himself admitted this point during a debate on the Act: 'It could be reasonably pointed out that a considerable number of people . . . would have been arrested under normal police powers if the Act had not been in force. What the section does is to strengthen, extend and perhaps in some cases *regularise* police powers of arrest and detention in relation to suspected terrorists' (our italics). After presenting recent arrest figures, he went on: 'Clearly most of these people would have been detained even if the Act had not been in force'.

Secondly, it is not acceptable to deprive someone of their liberty simply to obtain information from them if they are not suspected of any offence.

The extended period of detention has been justified by the need to check on a suspect's identity. Lord Shackleton stated in his report that associates need to be established and addresses verified, and that fingerprinting and photographing or the swabbing of hands or clothes for the traces of explosives 'all takes time'. Furthermore, other police forces, including the Royal Ulster Constabulary, may have to be consulted. Lord Shackleton pointed out how useful the extended period of detention under the Northern Ireland (Emergency Provisions) Act had been to the RUC – although that Act only permits 72 hours detention.

Lord Jellicoe thought that many terrorists had been trained in anti-interrogation techniques but that 'the interviewing officers may be able to build up a relationship with the suspect which removes his initial resistance and encourages him to talk, possibly on the fourth or fifth day in detention'.

The reality is that detention in custody is a punishment in itself and the suspect should therefore be charged as soon as possible, or released. The effect of extended periods of detention is in practice to induce the suspect to make a confession they might not otherwise have made, a statement which might incriminate themselves or others. The availability of long periods of detention for interrogation encourages the police to rely on confessions instead of independent evidence and hence undermines the principle that a suspect is innocent until *proved* guilty.

In theory, someone held under the Act is entitled to apply for a writ of *habeas corpus*. But this centuries-old remedy against unlawful detention has been nullified by the Prevention of Terrorism Act. By giving examining officers objectionably wide powers of arrest, and by making detention beyond 48 hours lawful with the Home Secretary's consent, the Act makes it impossible in practice to challenge the lawfulness of the detention. In any case, the courts have refused to treat such applications seriously. A habeas corpus application made on behalf of Paddy Prendeville in December 1979 was adjourned for four days!

A most unacceptable feature of the detention powers is the removal of basic safeguards for the suspect. Although in theory parts of the Judges Rules (and the Codes of Practice) apply to detentions under the Act, the only sanction for breach of the codes is that, in any subsequent trial, the judge may exclude a statement or confession obtained in breach of the code if the result is to make the statement unreliable. This sanction is inadequate since statements obtained in breach of the rules are regularly admitted in evidence. Moreover, it is completely irrelevant in the vast majority of arrests under the PTA as the people arrested are rarely charged or brought to court.

By allowing suspects to be held in complete isolation in the police station, compelled to submit to fingerprinting, photographing and forensic tests, possibly subject to abuse, intimidation or physical ill-treatment, the Prevention of Terrorism Act considerably increases the risk that the detainee will make a false confession to the police or make false allegations against someone else. The risk is increased with extended periods of detention. William Sargent, author of the seminal study *Battle of the Mind,* has explained that interrogators require six constant factors for 'successful' questioning: fatigue, tension, isolation, uncertainty, use of vicious language and a permeating atmosphere of seriousness. The Act's provisions and the virtual abolition of all normal safeguards make it difficult to regard as reliable confessions or statements obtained from those detained.

As illustrated by the Connolly case, all persons held under the Act are fingerprinted and photographed, 'reasonable force' being used where necessary. All photographs and fingerprints will be retained during the lifetime of the Act and are held in the national fingerprint collection at New Scotland Yard. This applies whether or not a person is released without charge or exclusion order. Apart from Connolly, no case is known of a successful application being made to destroy prints and photographs and, despite Connolly, the Metropolitan Police have subsequently refused to destroy prints taken from someone released without charge.

The danger of such records is that the fact of arrest under the Act will be used in future as grounds of suspicion against that person.

Conspiracy

Between November 1974 and December 1984, 13 people arrested under the Prevention of Terrorism Acts in Britain have been charged with conspiracy to commit an offence under the Acts, and others were charged with conspiracy to commit offences under other laws, for example 'conspiracy to possess explosives with intent to endanger life'. In Northern Ireland over the same period, the official statistics show 234 charges under the conspiracy laws.

The greatest injustice for defendants charged with conspiracy as opposed to other criminal offences, lies in differing rules of evidence in conspiracy trials. Although information which is intended to prove a defendant's membership of a particular conspiracy follows conventional rules of evidence, almost any piece of circumstantial information, however indirect, is allowed in to prove the existence of the conspiracy or agreement itself.

This meant in one case, for example, that literature found in a house (in which no-one was arrested) which carried the fingerprints of a co-defendant, was admitted as evidence. Literature, posters, correspondence or address books which illustrate the general political views of the defendant are admitted as a matter of course in proving the conspiracy. In addition, conspiracy charges can be vaguer, more 'flexible' and thus more difficult to refute. Normally, the indictment sets out in writing the core of the offence – that the person is charged with causing a particular explosion on the data and place mentioned. But conspiracy indictments can be very general, referring for instance to conspiracies to cause explosions over a two year period. Should the defendant be able to prove he or she was physically unable to 'conspire' during a year of this timespan, a conviction could still follow. As defence barrister Patrick O'Connor put it, 'Conspiracy charges are like an amoeba. You smash one part, but the rest stays alive'. This is, of course, not the case with charges for a substantive offence where an alibi covering the time of the crime ensures acquittal.

European Human Rights Convention

In December 1979, the Human Rights Commission declared admissible three cases brought by people who had been detained under the Act, Bernard McVeigh, Oliver O'Neill and Arthur Evans. In making that decision, the Commission accepted NCCL's argument that there is no 'domestic remedy' for alleged violations of the Convention arising from an arrest and detention under the Prevention of Terrorism Act. The Government had argued that the applications were inadmissible since none of the complaints had challenged the lawfulness of their detention by applying in the British courts for habeas corpus or making a claim for unlawful imprisonment.

Two of those who complained to the Commission were United Kingdom citizens; the third was Irish. On 22 February 1977, the three men arrived in Liverpool on the ferry from Dublin, having been on holiday together in Ireland. They were arrested and detained at a police station in Liverpool for 45 hours before being released without charge. They were searched, fingerprinted, photographed and questioned. They complained that they were not given proper reasons for their arrests, and two said that they were prevented from contacting their wives. The Government denied all the complaints, and said that the police had had information that at least one of the men had been involved 'in matters connected with terrorism'. The three men claimed that their detention was in breach of Article 5(i) of the Convention which states that no one shall be deprived of his or her liberty except in certain circumstances, none of which, they claimed, applied in this case. The Government claimed, however, that the detentions were justified as there was 'reasonable suspicion' that the men might have committed offences or be in the process of doing so. The Government also argued that, if someone was arrested because it was reasonably considered necessary to prevent a crime, Article 5 did not require 'reasonable suspicion'. It also asked the Commission to have regard to the background of terrorism against which the arrests had taken place.

The Commission began its judgement by noting that terrorism 'faces democratic governments with a problem of serious organised crime which they must cope with in order to preserve the fundamental rights of their citizens' but that the measures they take must comply with the Convention and that the Commission must 'always be alert to the danger of undermining or even destroying democracy on the ground of defending it.' Finally, although the Government stated that the arrests were because of suspicion that the men were involved in terrorism, the Commission noted that there was no evidence that they had been, and it had not even been alleged by the Government that they had. Nevertheless the Commission found that the Government was entitled to detain people for a security check at ports, because the examining officer thought it necessary on the basis of information available to him. The Government had argued that in practice the officials do not exercise their powers unless they have some suspicion and the Commission noted the conclusion in the Shackleton Report that their use of the powers was selective. The Commission concluded that there was no breach of Article 5 of the Convention.

Extension of the powers to cover 'international terrorism'

The Government's case for extending the arrest and detention powers to cover international terrorist suspects rested ostensibly on the recommendation to that effect from Lord Jellicoe. He considered that London 'could become a battleground for warring Middle East terrorist factions' (although he presented no evidence that this threat had increased nor that the police were unable to deal with it using the ordinary criminal law or immigration powers of deportation). The wording of the legislation does not, however, restrict the powers to acts of political violence related to international affairs committed *in* the United Kingdom as Jellicoe has implied. The Government acknowledged during the debates on the 1984 Bill that it had gone wider than Jellicoe in extending the powers to acts of terrorism committed anywhere in the world, whether or not they had any connection with the United Kingdom. Lord Elton, speaking for the Government, justified seeking these extensive powers by arguing that 'it is important that the UK should continue to take and should be seen to take a firm stand against terrorism in all its manifestations. Successive governments have strongly supported, advocated and pursued a policy of close co-operation with other countries to stamp out international terrorism. It is for this reason that we attach so much significance not only to the extension of the powers in regard to international terrorism but also to the absence of the territorial restriction . . . It would be wrong if by restricting the application of Clause 12 to acts of international terrorism committed in this country we lost the opportunity to show that our concern with terrorism is not limited to those of its manifestations which take place on our own soil or which directly affect our own subjects'.

At no time during any of the debates on this part of the Bill did the Government cite a single case in which the existing powers of the police had proved inadequate. Nor did it explain how it anticipated that the powers to detain people who could not be charged with any offence in this country might be used.

The arguments against the extension of the arrest and detention powers to cover 'international terrorism' were overwhelming. First, there was no evidence that international political violence in the UK had increased or was likely to do so. Indeed, the evidence suggested otherwise. Home Secretary William Whitelaw had responded to a parliamentary question in June 1982 in which he was asked whether there had been an increase in acts of terrorism within the Metropolitan area over the last ten years by saying: 'There does not appear to have been an increase in crimes connected with terrorism in this period.' NCCL examined the Metropolitan Police Commissioner's Annual Reports, and Her Majesty's Inspectorate of Constabulary Annual Reports for the previous three years and found few references to international terrorism and *no* indication at all that the police or Inspectorate felt that this was a growing or unmanageable problem for which more powers were needed. In NCCL's view the onus is on those who want extraordinary powers to show that they are needed, and this the Government failed to do. The police already have wide powers in the existing criminal law. Indeed Home Office Minister David Waddington (rejecting an attempt by a backbench Conservative MP to extend the powers even further (see 'Domestic Terrorism' below), said: 'We should not extend the emergency powers in the absence of clear evidence of a mischief that needs to be dealt with.'

Secondly there is no justification for extending the power to include those living peacefully here who may or may not be involved in political violence abroad, for example in liberation movements.

It is unacceptable in principle to detain people who are not suspected of any offence for which they could be charged in this country. (Most, but not all offences committed abroad are not triable here.) These 'suspects' could be deprived of their liberty for up to a week, presumably to obtain information. Of the 44 people arrested during the first nine months of the operation of the new Act, 13 (29.5%) were subsequently deported.

NCCL fears that the new power could be used indiscriminately, or more systematically on the basis of colour or other prejudice (for example against Libyans or Middle Eastern Arabs), to detain people from overseas in order to obtain information. Refugees, foreign students, black tourists or supporters of liberation or solidarity groups could now face detention and harassment.

Thirdly, although the English criminal law is generally, and quite properly, not concerned with prosecuting people for offences they commit abroad, there are a number of exceptions to this which already enable the police to detain people suspected of involvement in acts of violence abroad because these are offences for which they could be charged in this country. For example, a person can already be arrested and charged in this country if they are suspected of murdering a British citizen abroad or of conspiring to do so; of planning to use weapons abroad to endanger life or of conspiring to commit any crime abroad if they do anything unlawful here as part of their plan, e.g., forge documents.

The Government presented no evidence that these existing powers of arrest were inadequate. In response to considerable opposition to the new powers it did however promise to issue a circular to Chief Police Officers advising them to restrict their use of the powers. This circular (26/1984) was issued on 22 March 1984. It says that the powers should not be used in relation to acts of international terrorism 'unless either deportation is in prospect or it is thought that the involvement of the person concerned in such acts constitutes an offence under United Kingdom law. This restriction is likely to mean that, although the powers may be freely used in connection with acts of international terrorism committed in the UK, their use will rarely be justified in connection with acts of international terrorism committed outside the UK.' The circular lists the UK statutes which extend the jurisdiction of the UK courts to cover specific offences overseas (for which arrest under the PTA would thus be acceptable within the terms of the circular):

(i) Hijacking Act 1971
(ii) Protection of Aircraft Act 1973
(iii) Internationally Protected Persons Act 1973
(iv) Suppression of Terrorism Act 1978

(v) Taking of Hostages Act 1982
(vi) Nuclear Material (Offences) Act 1983
(vii) Tokyo Convention Act 1967 (piracy on the high seas)

In NCCL's view the use of a circular to restrict the use of these powers is unacceptable for the following reasons:

1. It is inappropriate for the Government to mitigate against the potential effects of a widely drawn section of an Act by giving ministerial assurances that it will in practice only be used in a more limited way. The correct course would have been for the Government to amend the Bill.

2. The assurances are not legally binding because:
   — if the political climate changes they could be withdrawn without reference to Parliament.
   — they cannot be relied upon by the judiciary in interpreting the law or the limits of police powers in individual cases.
   — the police have a statutory duty to enforce the law and cannot be instructed not to, hence the Home Secretary's 'advice'.

3. Even assuming the circular was observed, a future government may decide that it is 'conducive to the public good' for members of a particular liberation movement to be deported under the Immigration Act 1971 – perhaps under pressure from a 'friendly' foreign government. The police could then use these powers to detain the individuals *prior* to the deportation order being made. Under existing law they could not be detained for questioning until the deportation order had been made. The detention could thus be used to question the individual to obtain information to support the deportation order.

4. The circular assumes that the police will know before they make the arrest whether there is a possibility of a charge or deportation. This cannot always be the case. If the constable already has sufficient evidence to prefer charges the arrest should be made under the existing criminal law.

5. The grounds on which someone can be deported, that it will be 'conducive to the public good', are so wide that the limitation of the circular to those who could be deported is barely a restriction at all.

NCCL's fears that the new powers could be used indiscriminately are supported by paragraph 94 of the circular. In it, the Home Office reminds Chief Officers that the powers are exceptional and that Chief Officers will wish to take special precautions to ensure that all proprieties are observed 'to enable them to rebut allegations about abuse of power, for example that a person has been arrested for reasons connected with his political views or activities and not because he is suspected of being involved in terrorism'. It continues: *'This consideration will not be particularly important in cases involving the arrest of suspected international terrorists'!* (our emphasis).

NCCL has already advised a young student detained under these powers, when the police and customs officials involved appear to have breached the circular.

Milan Rai is an 18-year-old economics student at London University. He is Nepalese, has lived in the UK since he was nine and his father is in the British Army. In May 1984 he was returning from visiting a friend in France when he was detained by a customs official at Folkestone and held for two hours in police custody. He was told that he was being held under the PTA but never told why. He was too afraid to ask. He was stripped to his underclothes and his magazines and an address list were temporarily removed. The list, he was told, was taken to be photocopied. At no time was he questioned about *anything* related to any form of terrorism, any international (or Irish) organisation or indeed any crime. He was simply told that he could not expect to go through customs 'looking like that' (jeans and a T-shirt) carrying a load of 'anarchist shit' and that, if he did not co-operate, he would find himself 'going in the other direction' (deported). He was asked about his political views, CND and Greenham Common, and demonstrations he had been on; as well as the activities of his parents, brother and girlfriend. Despite the fact that his English is fluent he was frequently asked whether he understood English. He said afterwards that he felt the intention was to make him feel 'insulted, powerless and not part of English society'. He was refused permission to telephone the friend who was waiting for him.

Note on the 1976 Act

The wording of the 1976 Act actually permitted the arrest and detention of anyone suspected of involvement in terrorism *of any kind*. Although the Act was intended to relate to terrorism concerning Northern Ireland only, the arrest powers in the statute were not restricted in that way. According to the Government, this was necessary because a constable could not be expected, in an emergency, to find out whether the suspect was involved in terrorism concerning Northern Ireland, or some other cause, before deciding under which legislation to arrest them. The police were immediately advised by a Home Office circular to restrict their use of the powers to suspects in connection with Northern Ireland. They did not in fact always do so although the extent to which the circular was breached is not known as no separate statistics were kept. The fact that the wording of the 1976 Act included all kinds of terrorism led the Home Secretary initially to claim that the 1984 Act was more *restrictive,* now specifically excluding 'domestic terrorism'. However by the time the Bill reached the House of Lords the Government's spokesman acknowledged that the Bill, in practice, extended the powers by specifically including international terrorism.

Domestic Terrorism

The Section 12 and Section 13 arrest and detention powers do *not* cover people suspected of involvement in political violence solely connected with UK affairs other than Northern Ireland. Lord Jellicoe recommended that 'domestic terrorism' be excluded because he was not persuaded that the powers would be of real value and 'could prove counterproductive, by assisting such groups to gain a coherence and identity which they currently lack'.

A number of Conservative backbenchers sought to amend the Bill to include domestic terrorism. Harvey Proctor MP argued that 'logic demands that if we are to cover international and Northern Ireland terrorism, we should cover domestic terrorism'. He supported his case by listing a series of domestic terrorist incidents allegedly caused by Welsh and Scottish nationalists and an animal rights group. For the future he saw 'a severe and real danger for our capital city of London and our large cities and urban conurbations in the potential for terrorists to exploit racial tension. Black and white alike will try to exploit the position'. He concluded that there is a threat of domestic terrorism and that it would be 'sensible to insert the appropriate measure to combat it in the Bill now rather than wait until it happens and then try to plug the gap'.

In reply, the Government argued that the problem was not sufficiently serious to justify the extension of the powers. However, if at any time the problem changed, it 'would have no hesitation' in seeking approval of Parliament for an extension of the powers to suspected domestic terrorists as well.

The Act defines terrorism as the use of violence for political ends. The Government's reluctance to extend the powers to domestic political violence may be in part the result of anticipated difficulties the police would face in separating violence covered by the ordinary criminal law from that with a political motive.

Withholding information

What the Act says

Under Section 11, it is an offence not to pass on information to the police about a future act of terrorism or about people involved in terrorism occurring in the United Kingdom and connected with Northern Ireland affairs. 'Terrorism' is defined as the use of violence for political ends and includes any use of violence for the purpose of putting the public or any section of the public in fear.

A person who has information which he or she knows or believes might be of material assistance
(i) in preventing an act of terrorism related to Northern Ireland; or
(ii) in catching, prosecuting or convicting a person (other than him or herself) involved in terrorism, commits offences if he or she fails to pass on the information to the police (unless he or she had a reasonable excuse not to do so). (In Northern Ireland the information can be passed on to a member of the Armed Forces.)

It is not an offence for an individual to refuse to give information about *themselves* but it is an offence for wives or husbands to refuse to pass on such information about their spouses. A person can be charged in any place they have visited since the time that they obtained the information.

Maximum penalties: on conviction in the magistrates' court, a fine of £2000 and/or six months' imprisonment, or if the case is heard in the Crown Court, an unlimited fine and/or five years' imprisonment.

The police cannot arrest someone they suspect of this offence under the PTA itself but it remains an arrestable offence under the ordinary criminal law, because it carries a prison sentence of up to five years.

The record

An examination of the statistics on the number of prosecutions under Section 11 shows that the section has been little used in

Britain. Up until 31 December 1984, a total of 15 people had been charged in Britain with withholding information of which two cases were not proceeded with. Of those remaining, ten were found guilty and three acquitted; eight received suspended sentences and two were sent to prison for less than a year.

Lord Jellicoe found in his inquiry that the main purpose of this provision is not to secure the maximum number of convictions, but to persuade people to talk. The individual's knowledge that he or she could be prosecuted may fulfill the police's objective – to induce the person to give information – so that the question of prosecution does not often arise.

In Northern Ireland, 71 people have been charged under Section 11 up to 3 December 1984. There is a general practice there to prefer a charge of 'concealing information' against individuals also charged with more serious offences so that, failing a conviction for the more serious charge, the person may still be found guilty of the lesser offence.

Lord Jellicoe's arguments centred on the need to encourage terrorists – or their relatives or acquaintances – to talk. However, he found that the section is also commonly used to make the *victims* of terrorist crimes provide information which they are too afraid to give, for instance if their car is hijacked. A case which arose from the Maze breakout in October 1983 illustrates how this section can force an innocent victim to choose between prosecution under Section 11 or reprisals from the paramilitaries.

The *Sunday Times* reported on 9 October that the RUC were protecting the home of Ian and Doreen MacFarland in County Down after they had been held hostage by eight of the prisoners who escaped from the Maze. It was previously reported that the prisoners had forced the MacFarlands to swear on the Bible that they would not go to the police for three days and that they had subsequently been advised by their local Minister not to break that promise. The *Sunday Times* quoted RUC sources as saying that Mr MacFarland was likely to be charged for withholding information. The fact that the RUC were protecting the home indicates their recognition that the MacFarlands were in danger fo reprisals.

Finally, Section 11 has been used in a way which was never even considered, far less intended, when it was first introduced in 1976 – to censor the media. Here again it has been the threat of prosecution which has achieved the apparent objective: to prevent journalists recording the views and actions of the paramilitaries.

The use of Section 11 to censor the press was not envisaged when the power was introduced in 1976. It was, however, wholeheartedly endorsed by the Government when opposed by Labour MPs during the passage of the 1984 Bill.

In July 1979, a BBC *Tonight* interview with a member of the

INLA provoked press and political comment that the BBC lacked 'judgement'; that its decision was in 'bad taste'. The subsequent filming of an IRA roadblock by the *Panorama* team at Carrickmore in October 1979 drew a similar reaction that the BBC was 'giving publicity to terrorists'.

In response, in November 1979, the DPP asked Scotland Yard to investigate whether the journalists in either incident had committed an offence under Section 11; that is, the decision to broadcast the views and actions of the paramilitaries, itself not an offence, led to consideration of the use of legislation intended for a different purpose.

The Attorney General reported the results of the investigation to the House of Commons on 1 August 1980. He had, he said, decided not to prosecute but said that he 'was satisfied that the actions of the BBC staff were of a kind that would have constituted offences under Section 11 of the 1976 Act'.

We understand that the basis of the prosecutions would have been that the journalists failed to notify the police of the arrangements for the interviews/filming and of the identity of those with whom they made the arrangements, in advance.

The Attorney General informed the Commons that he had told the BBC that:

'If similar incidents took place again I would take a stricter view of what had happened and those who participated would be on warning that, subject to the evidence and circumstances of the case, they risk criminal proceedings under the Prevention of Terrorism (Temporary Provisions) Act'.

The BBC released their correspondence with the Attorney General who had written to them that the two incidents 'constituted little more than propaganda exercises by terrorist organisations to which your staff have willingly given their support'. This letter reinforces the view that it was not the 'prevention of terrorism' but the 'prevention of the reporting of terrorism' which was at issue.

Of particular concern is the Attorney General's statement that:

'Any interview with a person purporting to represent a terrorist organisation is potentially a source of information of the nature referred to in Section 11 of the Act arising not only from the actual contents of the interview but also from any negotiations leading up to and the actual arrangements for it'.

Sir Michael Swann, Chairman of the BBC Governors, replied:

'This last phrase could be read as meaning that the police should be informed, at every turn, of the letters, phone calls or meetings with go-betweens which are, I have no doubt, necessary if a journalist is ever to acquire information from known or suspected terrorists. If this is really what the law says, then all reporting of who the terrorists are and what they say would, in practice, be halted abruptly'.

On 4 August 1980 the Attorney General confirmed that the BBC had interpreted his statement accurately.

It is unclear whether the Attorney General would ever prosecute a journalist under Section 11, given the controversy about press freedom which would ensue. But the *threat* of prosecution has itself effectively curtailed reporting on the Northern Ireland conflict.

The BBC necessarily cited Section 11 in its next edition of its journalists' handbook, the *News and Current Affairs Index,* as a legal consideration which journalists should take into account. So far as is known, neither the BBC nor the IBA have given permission for the filming of interviews with spokespersons for the IRA or INLA, or of their activities, since the Attorney General's ruling.

Against Section 11

This section originated with former MP George Cunningham whose arguments the Government accepted. He said: 'the situation in practice is more likely to be that a prosecution is brought against ten people, for example, for a given outrage, two of them being charged with committing the act and conspiring to do it, and the others being charged formally only with conspiracy. It may be that the jury is satisfied that some of the accused did it and some of them conspired to do it. The jury may, on the evidence, be satisfied that those persons knew about it and could have informed the police. I suggest that this is a realistic scenario. As the law stands, the people found to have knowledge but who did not conspire could not be convicted of anything. I suggest that there is a situation which we should remove'.

George Cunningham later argued that a person charged with a substantial offence and/or with conspiracy should also be subject to a charge of 'concealing information', thus enabling a jury which did not convict on the heavier charge to do so on the lesser one. This is a general practice in Northern Ireland. Cunningham likened this section to a provision that already exists in the Criminal Law Act 1967, whereby it is an offence to accept a bribe for not giving relevant information to the police. Political motivation, he argued, can be as important as financial reward to the potential offender.

Lord Shackleton expressed grave doubts about Section 11, both on grounds of principle and about the way it could be used in the course of interviewing. He added 'It has in any case been little used in Great Britain, and the obvious difficulties of proof may be a factor in this respect. . . Section 11 was not thought necessary in 1974. It has an unpleasant ring about it in terms of civil liberties'. He therefore recommended that it be allowed to lapse forthwith.

During the 1979 debate Merlyn Rees, then Home Secretary, concluded that for the time being the section should not be dropped, but added that the position would be reviewed in a year's time. During the March 1980 renewal debate, William Whitelaw stated: 'I have consulted the police, who are firmly of the view that Section 11 is an important weapon in the struggle against terrorism . . . Having considered the matter very carefully, I have concluded that Section 11 should be retained'. The Act was subsequently renewed with Section 11 intact.

Lord Jellicoe accepted police evidence to his inquiry that on a number of occasions an individual's knowledge that they were liable to prosecution if they failed to provide such information was a major if not vital factor in persuading them to do so. He concluded that 'the Section is of significant value to the police service but that the service could operate without it if required to do so'. He recommended that Section 11 should remain because its value 'is not outweighed by the arguments of principle against it'.

Opposition peers, during the debates on the 1984 Bill did not agree. For the first time, Labour and Liberal peers united in an attempt to have the Section removed from the Bill. They forced a vote during the Report stage which the Government won with 129 votes to 92. Lord Denning had argued, in support of the Government, that 'it is a matter of justice to the community as a whole. An individual who withholds information that could save lives is quite properly to be brought before the court.'

Section 11 represents a dangerous innovation and, in conjunction with the police powers of arrest and detention, could lead to suspects giving false and misleading information to obtain an early release from police custody.

The effect of Section 11 is to undermine an individual's right to remain silent during questioning. Lord Jellicoe rejected this criticism, recommending only that the wording of the Section be amended (as it has) to clarify that the individual is not required to provide information about himself or herself. He insisted that the right not to provide information about oneself amounted to the right to silence.

However, the wording of the right to silence ('You are not obliged to say anything unless you wish to do so') is intentionally wider for good reason. The information which a suspect is forced to give about others can clearly simultaneously implicate him or her. Under Section 11 people can be prosecuted for failing to give information about others which could also incriminate themselves in the same or related offences.

Lord Jellicoe recognised that the greatest potential for abuse of this power was at the interrogation stage, for example, pressurising a relative who inadvertently picked up information, with consequent divided loyalties or fear of reprisals. Lord Shackleton had also noted that 'there is a distinction between suspicion and sure knowledge, and that where a person merely suspects that someone may be involved in terrorism but has no certain knowledge, he might understandably be wary of implicating someone who might be quite innocent'.

The use of Section 11 to curb journalists' freedom was raised in Parliament during the debates on the 1984 Bill. Clive Soley MP argued that 'the issue becomes one of the freedom of the press and other media to report on events as they deem appropriate' and Gerald Bermingham MP asked the Minister whether he would not agree that 'if journalism is truly accurate it can clearly and effectively display the abhorrent beliefs, practices and acts of perpetrators of terrorist offences and that, in its own way, that is beneficial to society because the true nature of what is being done is thereby demonstrated'. But the Home Office Minister David Waddington dismissed their concern, arguing that: 'It is hard to believe that people in this country will have any sympathy with the criticism that it inhibits the media from giving publicity to terrorists, their causes and their methods. It is absurd to suggest that there should not be some restrictions on press freedom when the saving of life is at issue'.

NCCL believes that Section 11 should not be used against journalists because:

(i) This was not the intention of the 1976 Act and there was no evidence presented during the course of the 1983 Bill on either the desirability or necessity of restricting journalists' freedom in relation to Northern Ireland.

(ii) It is essential that the public throughout the UK understand fully the nature and causes of the conflict in Northern Ireland, including the views of the paramilitaries. Censorship of these views inhibits such understanding and consequently the search for a lasting political solution.

(iii) Freedom of the press is an essential civil liberty which should be guarded jealously. As the NUJ argued in a letter to the Home Secretary asking that Section 11 be removed from the

1984 Bill, 'There is no evidence to suggest that this form of censorship has helped in any way to reduce the level of violence in Northern Ireland'. We agree with the NUJ view that, on the contrary, 'the removal of Section 11 would go some way, at least, towards the creation of a climate in which helpful discussion of the Northern Ireland question – including some insight into the thinking of those who have used murder and violence – could take place in the interests of finding a solution to the problem'.

The use of the Acts in Northern Ireland

by Dermot Walsh

The PTA as part of a web of emergency legislation

In some respects the Prevention of Terrorism (Temporary Provisions) Acts (PTA) carry a higher profile among the Irish community in Britain than they do in Northern Ireland. That is not to suggest that the legislation is not applicable to Northern Ireland. On the contrary, it applies there almost to the same extent as it does in the rest of the United Kingdom.[1] More than that, the statistics reveal that the incidence of arrests under the Acts is much higher there than in Britain.[2] How is it then that it is the Irish in Britain who are more likely to be aware of its existence? The answer lies primarily in the fact that when people in Britain are subjected to such extreme powers they will readily identify the PTA as their source. This is because the coercive powers contained in that legislation are so unlike any other powers which they are familiar with.

For people in Northern Ireland the experience is radically different. They have grown up with such measures. The existence and use of virtually uncontrollable executive powers are and always have been the norm there. From the establishment of Northern Ireland as an entity in 1922 until the present day, the executive authorities have enjoyed very broad, almost untrammelled powers.[3] These have ranged from a minister's power to intern without trial to a soldier's power to arrest without reasonable suspicion. While the finer wording and details have varied at different periods the substantive content of the powers has not. For people living in republican and working class areas they have always meant an almost total subjection to executive authority. Their freedom of movement, freedom of expression, freedom of thought, freedom of association, right to liberty and right to bodily integrity have always depended not on the due process of law but on the whim of an official, whether a soldier, policeman, prison officer, civilian searcher, civil servant or minister.

The feeling of helplessness engendered by the content of these powers is fuelled by the bewildering complexity of their sources. They are contained in a sizeable number of statutes and statutory instruments the titles of which have varied over time. They began with the Civil Authorities (Special Powers) Act (N.I.), 1922, which was re-enacted annually until 1928, when it was enacted for five years' duration; and then it was made permanent in 1933. This was supplemented by numerous statutory instruments made by the Northern Ireland Minister for Home Affairs under powers conferred by the Act. Further gross infringements of civil liberties and human rights were contained in the Flags and Emblems Act (Northern Ireland) Act, 1954, the Criminal Justice (Temporary Provisions) Act (N.I.) 1970, as amended in 1971, and the Firearms Act (Northern Ireland), 1969, as amended in 1971. The Civil Authorities (Special Powers) Act and its progeny were repealed in 1973 only to be replaced by the Northern Ireland (Emergency Provisions) Act 1973 followed by the Prevention of Terrorism (Temporary Provisions) Acts of 1974 and 1976, the Northern Ireland (Emergency Provisions) Act, the EPA Act 1978 and the Prevention of Terrorism Act 1984. It was the EPA which introduced the non-jury Diplock Courts for terrorist-type offences and relaxed the rules of evidence for these offences to allow the admissibility in court of involuntary confessions.

This collection of legislation is responsible for the blanket of emergency powers which has covered Northern Ireland since its birth. The PTA, obviously, is only a part of this apparatus, and by no means an exceptional part. Most, if not all, of its provisions have appeared in other statutes some of which are still in force. So, not only are the provisions of the PTA 'old hat' to the populace of Northern Ireland but, in some respects, they duplicate powers already available. It is hardly surprising, therefore, that the PTA does not carry a very high profile in Northern Ireland. Anyone subjected to one of its provisions is unlikely to identify it as the source of his or her trouble. On the contrary, it will appear as simply another thread in the extensive web of repressive powers available to the state authorities. Indeed, even the state authorities themselves find difficulty in identifying which brand of emergency laws they are acting under. The author was stopped and questioned at a U.D.R. (Ulster Defence Regiment) checkpoint on the North-east Antrim coast in the early hours of a Sunday morning in the summer of 1983. On asking what powers they were operating under a soldier replied that it was the Special Powers Act; an Act that was repealed in 1973! The power they were really exercising – even if they did not know it – was Section 18 of the Northern Ireland (Emergency Provisions) Act 1978. If the beneficiaries of these extensive powers find difficulty in distinguishing between them in a given situation it is hardly surprising that the victim should experience similar difficulty.

Simply because the PTA does not carry as high a profile in Northern Ireland as it may among the Irish community in Britain it does not follow that it has little impact. On the contrary, the fact that it can hide behind the corporate veil of emergency powers there means that it can avoid, to a much greater extent than in Britain, the public scrutiny and denunciation that it deserves. Indeed, when used in conjunction with other emergency provisions it becomes positively brutal. It renders its victims even more helpless than is the case in Britain. This can be seen most clearly in the context of a criminal trial.

The PTA and trial by special court

International law and all civilised nations recognise the fundamental right of an individual to be presumed innocent until proved guilty in the course of a fair trial.[4] The authorities in Northern Ireland, however, by using section 12 of the PTA in conjunction with the EPA are denying many people their basic right to a fair trial. This can be illustrated by the treatment of all those arrested under section 12 of the PTA and tried in Northern Ireland's special 'Diplock' courts, (under the EPA) in the first three months of 1981.[5]

For most of them the ordeal began with their being arrested by a contingent of policemen and soldiers who called at their homes around five o'clock in the morning. They were taken immediately to Castlereagh and Gough holding centres. This is highly significant because these centres are no ordinary police stations. They were specially constructed in 1976-77 to facilitate the government's switch from a policy of detention without trial to that of channelling suspects through special courts. This required securing evidence and that is where Castlereagh and Gough come in. They were designed specifically for the purpose of conducting police interrogation in a highly organised, efficient and productive manner;[6] productive in this context means confessions which could be used subsequently to secure convictions in the special courts.

Everything about these centres is aimed at producing a steady flow of confessions from suspects. The British government's committee of inquiry into interrogation procedures described their physical conditions as 'austere and forbidding'.[7] The regime operated there is equally severe. Between them the centres have no less than 30 specially-designed interrogation rooms. These allow the RUC to conduct a large number of interrogations simultaneously. The normal routine is to subject each suspect to repetitive interrogation sessions by rotating teams of detectives. In any one day there could be four or five of these sessions, each lasting about two hours. The inevitable effect of such intensive interrogation carried out by unfriendly detectives in such a lonely and alien environment is the exhaustion, disorientation and intimidation of the suspect. The longer it is continued the more likely it will be that the suspect will grasp at any straw to escape; this can mean confessing whatever it is the detectives want him or her to confess to.

This is where Section 12 of the PTA plays such a crucial role. A suspect arrested under this provision is faced with the prospect of up to seven days of such treatment. One can imagine that after the first day he or she will have little stomach for the remaining six. It is to be expected, therefore, that confessions would be readily forthcoming. And that is exactly what happens. Of the 17 individuals arrested under Section 12 and tried in the special court in the first three months of 1981, fourteen were alleged to have made a confession under police interrogation. A very significant feature about them is that only one had been arrested in suspicious circumstances. In other words only one of them has an obvious motivation for confessing which was not directly related to the method of interrogation.

Although these suspects were alleged to have made confessions, that did not ensure them a speedy trial. The average time interval between arrest and trial was 14 months which, for the vast majority, was spent in custody. It is worth remembering here that Article 6(i) of the European Convention on Human Rights regards a speedy trial as being a primary ingredient of a fair trial.

When they eventually reached the courtroom these suspects found that the scales of justice had been almost irreversibly weighted against them as a result of their arrest and interrogation under Section 12 of the PTA, and their trial in a non-jury court allowing involuntary confessions. If they had been tried in a British court there would have been an onus on the prosecution to prove beyond any reasonable doubt that their confessions had been extracted voluntarily, i.e. without fear of prejudice or hope of advantage held out by someone in authority or by oppression.[8] If they failed to establish that the confession was voluntary then it would at least in theory, be inadmissible as evidence of the accused's guilt. This is intended to prevent the police from pre-empting the result of the trial by applying improper pressure on the suspect to confess his or her guilt while in their custody. In other words it should ensure that the issue of the accused's innocence or guilt is determined in the courtrooms and not in the police station. While British judges in practice often fail to exclude involuntary confessions, reported cases in which confessions have been ruled inadmissible because involuntary illustrate how invaluable and fundamental a protection this is.[9] Perhaps the most significant of these for present purposes are two Northern Ireland cases which occurred in 1972 before the PTA and the EPA were enacted: *R. v. Flynn and Leonard*[10] and *R. v. Gargan*.[11] Those concerned confessions made by the accuseds in the course of interrogation by the RUC in Palace Barracks, a predecessor of Castlereagh and Gough. The confessions had not been obtained by physical ill-treatment but by a regime which was 'officially organised and operated in order to obtain information from persons who would otherwise have been less willing to give it.'[12] According to the Lord Chief Justice that in itself was sufficient to render the confessions inadmissible.

Applying the above principle it would seem that confessions obtained in Castlereagh and Gough should be automatically inadmissible. And so they would be if it was not for the special rules of evidence which apply in the special court under the EPA; rules which make it difficult to acquit an accused who arrives in the court having made a confession in Castlereagh or Gough. They declare that all confessions may be admitted in evidence if they are relevant and if the prosecution can establish, when called upon to do so, that they were not obtained by torture, inhuman or degrading treatment.[13] This effectively gives RUC interrogators almost *carte blanche* to use whatever methods they wish, short of torture, inhuman and degrading treatment to extract confessions from suspects. They have in fact developed interrogation techniques including: repetitive, intensive and exhaustive interrogation sessions with little time in between for rest; including disorientation by adopting aggressive and friendly interrogation styles in quick succession; threatening to re-arrest continually until a confession is forthcoming; threatening to arrest and charge his or her parents, brothers, sisters etc.; threatening to have his or her children taken into care; threatening to spread the word that he or she is an informer; offering him or her bribes and support and subjecting him or her to verbal abuse and ridicule.[14] The danger is that a suspect may choose to risk making a suitable 'confession' rather than suffer this treatment for seven days with the probability that the treatment will be repeated again and again in the future. But the special rules of evidence combined with the special powers of arrest and the special interrogation procedures all rail-road the accused towards conviction. Nor does the accused even have the safeguard of a jury determining guilt or innocence as the case will be heard by a judge alone.[15]

It is indicative of just how unfair trial in the Diplock court is that confessions extracted by such methods are treated as reliable and acceptable evidence. All those in the sample who confessed after being interrogated in Castlereagh and Gough under Section 12 were convicted. With the exception of one they all received custodial sentences.

The RUC are effectively encouraged to use Section 12 of the PTA as an aid to extracting confessions by the fact that the authorities are happy to prefer charges on the basis of those confessions. The authorities for their part, are happy to prefer charges because they feel confident that they will be accepted in the Diplock court, despite the fact that they have been obtained by a much harsher regime than that used by the British police. This is reflected in the statistics which show an increasing preference on the part of the RUC to arrest under Section 12 and the fact that these arrests result in much higher rate of charges in Northern Ireland than in Britain.[16]

Exclusion orders

The remaining provisions of the Act are open to the same criticisms as apply to their operation in Britain. However, it is worth drawing special attention to the use of exclusion orders and port detentions on persons travelling from Northern Ireland to Britain. The official justification for these powers is the desire to take stern preventive measures to thwart potential terrorist activity. One is entitled to presume that the government is committed to protecting all citizens of the United Kingdom against such activity. The operation of exclusion orders, however, would suggest that this commitment is a very selective one. The statistics reveal that the traffic is virtually all one way – from Britain to Northern Ireland. If every person served with an exclusion order is really a terrorist then the British government is buying greater peace and security for Britain at the expense of Northern Ireland which is being reduced to a convenient detention area for terrorists who, for some reason, cannot be locked up.

It is doubtful, however, that such persons are really terrorists. Indeed, it is virtually unheard of for such individuals to be arrested and charged with terrorist offences on their return to Northern Ireland. Indeed many believe a more likely explanation for their being treated as *personae non grata* is their political convictions and activities. Many of them identify with working class, community and radical groups which are highly critical of government policy in Northern Ireland. It has been alleged that exclusion is used to prevent these people from publicising their views about the British presence in Northern Ireland; the exclusion of Gerry

Adams, preventing him from addressing meetings in Britain, could only give substance to that view.

Conclusion

When Parliament first enacted the PTA in 1974 it did so with the minimum of debate. Essentially it was sold as a measure necessary to deal with a possible IRA campaign in Britain. No explanation was ever given as to why it was thought necessary to include Northern Ireland within its ambit. At that stage Northern Ireland was already overburdened with emergency powers, police and soldiers. The last thing it needed was another helping of the same. Little thought, if any, was devoted to the question of how the provisions of the PTA would operate within the emergency system of criminal justice in force there. There is no evidence to suggest that the authorities were alive to the danger that the PTA would prove an even greater monster when used in conjunction with other emergency powers than it would when functioning in the context of an ordinary criminal justice system. Certainly the two official inquiries into the operation of the PTA did not devote any space to the danger.[17] Neither Lord Shackleton nor Lord Jellicoe saw fit to investigate and consider the justice of arresting and interrogating a suspect under Section 12 of the PTA and then trying him or her in the special court. They confined themselves to the terms of the PTA itself.

It was not until 1980 that the RUC began in earnest to use Section 12 in combination with the other emergency apparatus. Having been pressed to abandon the practice of using physical force to extract confessions from suspects in their custody they needed a replacement,[18] and they found it in Section 12.[19] With the power to detain a suspect for up to seven days they could break the suspect's resistance down indirectly by long, drawn out, oppressive interrogation sessions, or the threat of them.

To date it would appear that the authorities are not opposed to this unintended and unplanned-for development. Indeed, if Sir George Baker's report is implemented they will actively encourage it.[20] He conducted an official inquiry into the operation of the Northern Ireland (Emergency Provisions) Act 1978 which finally considered the relationship between the two sets of emergency provisions. Unfortunately his treatment of the relationship was neither comprehensive nor searching. He did not even see fit to investigate the fairness of trial in the special court following arrest and interrogation under Section 12. The implication of his recommendations, however, is that he sees nothing unfair or unjust about this. Naïvely basing his knowledge of arrest and interrogation on the RUC version to the exclusion of all other accounts he concludes that it is quite safe to leave a suspect in RUC custody for up to seven days.[21] There is nothing new in this approach, however. It has become quite normal for the people of Northern Ireland to be subjected to treatment which would never be tolerated in Britain. One can almost forgive Sir George, therefore, for imagining that a rationalisation of the emergency provisions constitutes progress. It does, however, leave a sense of despair that the authorities will never realise that emergency legislation is simply part of the on-going saga in Northern Ireland and not part of its solution.

Footnotes

1. Part 1 does not apply to Northern Ireland.
2. In comparing the statistics one must take into account the massive differential in population size.
3. See Walsh: 'Civil Liberties in Northern Ireland' in *Civil Liberties 1984* ed. Peter Wallington (Martin Robertson, 1984).
4. The Universal Declaration of Human Rights, adopted by the General Assembly of the United Nations on 10 December, 1948, Arts. 10, 11; The European Convention on Human Rights, Art. 6.
5. There were 17 such persons. A complete survey was carried out on all those who had been tried in the special court in the first three months of 1981. For the results and analysis of this see: Walsh: *The Use and Abuse of Emergency Legislation in Northern Ireland* (The Cobden Trust, 1984).
6. *Report of the Committee of Inquiry into Police Interrogation Procedures in Northern Ireland* (HMSO 1979, Cmnd. 7497) (The Bennett Report) paras. 46-54; Peter Taylor: *Beating the Terrorists? Interrogation in Omagh, Gough and Castlereagh.*
7. Bennett report para. 49.
8. *DPP v. Ping Lin* [1976] AC 475.
9. Cross: *Evidence* (Butterworth, 5th ed. 1979), pp. 539-541.
10. [1972] NIJB
11. Ibid.
12. Ibid.
13. Northern Ireland (Emergency Provisions) Act 1978, section 8.
14. See Walsh, infra. pp. 56-78.
15. Northern Ireland (Emergency Provisions) Act 1978, section 7.
16. See appendix.
17. HMSO 1978 (Cmnd. 7324); HMSO 1983 (Cmnd. 8803)
18. International and internal pressure forced the government to set up an official inquiry into RUC interrogation procedures in 1979 (the Bennett inquiry). That signalled the end of the practice of using physical force on suspects in RUC custody. For detail on such practices see: Peter Taylor, infra.
19. It is significant that from 1980 onwards RUC use of the powers under Section 12 increased dramatically, and is still rising.
20. *Review of the Operation of the Northern Ireland (Emergency Provisions) Act 1978* (HMSO 1984, Cmnd. 9222) (The Baker Report) paras. 267, 273, 279, 283, 285, 300.
21. Ibid. Paras. 262-313.

Conclusion

The Prevention of Terrorism Acts have severely undermined the principles of natural justice and the rule of law. Their provisions violate international standards on human rights – standards accepted by the British Government itself. The following points summarise the most disturbing effects of the Acts.

1. By giving the Home Secretary the power to authorise detention for up to seven days without access to a court, the Act has destroyed *habeas corpus* as a safeguard against unlawful detention.

2. The Act authorises detention for questioning. A detainee need not be suspected of any specific offence: arrest and detention can be based on 'reasonable' suspicion of involvement in 'terrorism' generally. For detention at ports of entry – where the majority occur – officers do not need any suspicion at all of involvement in terrorism.

3. The power to exclude a United Kingdom citizen from one part of the country to another has given the Home Secretary the right to impose arbitrary, executive punishment on the basis of secret evidence. Suspects have no right to know or challenge the evidence against them and no right to a court hearing. The exclusion order provision is probably a breach of the European Human Rights Convention (which guarantees the right to a fair hearing); furthermore, its continued existence makes it impossible for the United Kingdom to ratify Protocol 4 of the Convention (which protects the right of citizens to freedom of movement within their own country).

4. The power to ban organisations by executive decision, coupled with vague provisions about support for proscribed organisations or for terrorism generally, severely undermine freedom of association and freedom to express views which conflict with Government policy.

5. The extension of the Acts in 1984 to cover 'international terrorism' allows the police to detain, for up to seven days, people who are not suspected of any crime in the United Kingdom and could not be charged with any offence. They would be detained solely for information gathering.

Like the old Special Powers Acts, the Prevention of Terrorism Act means that 'individual liberty is no longer protected by law, but is at the arbitrary disposition of the Executive'. Protests from the United Kingdom about human rights violations abroad come ill from a government which demands such excessive powers for itself. The United Kingdom Government and the British press and large sections of the British public condemned the Soviet Government's 'internal exile' of Sakharov and other dissidents. But a system of internal exile is precisely what the Prevention of Terrorism Act has created for the United Kingdom.

Appendix 1: Statistics

Summary of the operation of the Acts in Great Britain and Northern Ireland, 29 November 1974 - 31 December 1984.

Contents

Summary of the operation of the Acts in
Great Britain and Northern Ireland
29 November 1974 - 31 December 1984

1. Detentions under the Acts in Great Britain relating to Northern Ireland

a)

Total detained	At port/ airport	Elsewhere
5,905	4,175 (70.7%)	1,730 (29.3%)

b)

Total detained	Charged with any offence	Not charged with any offence
5,905	459 (7.8%)	5,446 (92.2%)

c)

Total detained	Charged with any offence	Exclusion order made	Not charged or excluded
5,905	459 (7.7%)	275 (4.7%)	5,171 (87.6%)

2. Detentions under the Acts in Great Britain relating to international terrorism (1984 Act only)

a)

Total detained	At port/ airport	Elsewhere
44	5 (11.4%)	39 (88.6%)

b)

Total detained	Deported	Charged with any offence	Not charged with any offence or deported
44	13 (29.5%)	8 (18.2%)	23 (52.3%)

3. Total detentions under the Acts in Great Britain: by police force area

Metropolitan Police	1,280
Merseyside	1,364
Dumfries and Galloway	1,222
Other (England and Wales)	1,768
Other (Scotland)	315
Total	5,949

4. Exclusion Orders

a)

Exclusion order applied for in Great Britain	Orders refused	Orders made
358	48	310

b)

Orders Made	Person removed from Great Britain to:		Already outside Great Britain	Revoked before removal	Removal to Northern Ireland under other powers
	N. Ireland	Republic			
310	245	40	13	11	1

c)

Person removed from N. Ireland
30

5. *Detention period in Great Britain of all those not charged with any offence or excluded.*

	1983	1984
More than 1 hour and less than 2 hours	1	1
2 hours and less than 4	3	6
4 hours and less than 8	9	7
8 hours and less than 12	13	8
12 hours and less than 24	43	41
24 hours and less than 36	26	49
36 hours and less than 48	27	27
Total under 48 hours	122	139
2 days and less than 3	11	1
3 days and less than 4	7	4
4 days and less than 5	0	4
5 days and less than 6	0	1
6 days and less than 7	7	9
7 days	0	0
Total 48 hours or more	25	19
Total detained but not charged or excluded	147	158

NB: These figures do not include people charged with an offence or served with an exclusion order, who are *more* likely to have been held for over 48 hours.

6. *Detention period in Great Britain of all those detained in connection with international terrorism beyond 48 hours*

	Persons detained
3 days	1
4 days	0
5 days	5
6 days	0
7 days	12
Total number of persons whose detention was extended beyond 48 hours (2 days)	18
Out of a total number detained in connection with international terrorism	44

7. *Detentions under the Acts in Northern Ireland 1974-1984*

	Persons detained
1974 (from 29 November)	–
1975	8
1976	246
1977	162
1978	155
1979	162
1980	222
1981	495
1982	828
1983	1174
1984	908
Total	4360

8. *Detentions under the Acts in Northern Ireland by outcome*

Total detentions	Excluded	Charged with offence under Acts	Charged with other offences
4,360	30 (0.7%)	91 (2.1%)	1652 (37.9%)

9. *Extension of detention beyond 48 hours in Northern Ireland*

Applications for Extension	Extension granted	Extension refused	Application withdrawn	Extension less than 5 days	Extension more than 5 days
3,110	3,087	4	19	166	2,921

10. Persons charged under the PTA in Great Britain and Northern Ireland 29 November 1974 - 31 December 1984

	Great Britain	N. Ireland
Sections 1 and 2 (soliciting or receiving money for a proscribed organisation or displaying support for such an organisation).	10	(Not applicable. S1 and S2 only apply in Britain. In Northern Ireland these acts are offences under the Emergency Provisions (Northern Ireland) Act 1978
Sections 9 (1) and 9 (2) (a) (Failure to comply with an exclusion order and helping an excluded person to breach the order).	18	8
Sections 10 (1) and 10 (2) (contributions to acts of terrorism)	54	11
Section 11 (withholding information)	15	71
Section 3 (Failure to co-operate with examination at port)	55	—
Article 13 (3) of the Prevention of Terrorism (Supplemental Temporary Provisions) (NI) Order 1976 (Aircraft landing without approval)	—	1

11. Persons stopped at ports in England & Wales under the PTA

1979	1980	1981	1982	1983	1984
41,936	48,090	No figures available	44,704	44,906	47,779

Telephone enquiries concerning   Searches made under the PTA
possible suspect terrorist
made to the National
Joint Unit

Source of Statistics

Home Office statistics on the operation of the Prevention of Terrorism (Temporary Provisions) Acts 1974, 1976 and 1984 – Fourth Quarter 1984 (30 January 1985).

Northern Ireland Information Service Prevention of Terrorism (Temporary Provisions) Acts 1974, 1976 and 1984 – Statistics for the Fourth Quarter of 1984 (24 January 1985). NB. The Northern Ireland Statistics are less comprehensive than the Home Office statistics and it has not therefore been possible to include comparable statistics for Northern Ireland in all cases.

'Report of Her Majesty's Chief Inspector of Constabulary' 1979-84.

PREVENTION OF TERRORISM (TEMPORARY PROVISIONS) ACT 1984

EXCLUSION ORDER

Whereas I am satisfied that

is attempting or may attempt to enter Great Britain with a view to

being concerned in the commission, preparation or instigation of

acts of terrorism designed to influence public opinion or Government policy

with respect to affairs in Northern Ireland:

And whereas it has not been shown that the said

is a British citizen:

Now, therefore, in pursuance of section 6(1) and (2) of the Prevention of

Terrorism (Temporary Provisions) Act 1984 I, by this order,

prohibit the said

from being in, or entering, the United Kingdom

And in pursuance of Article 9(3) of the Prevention of Terrorism

(Supplemental Temporary Provisions) Order 1984 I hereby authorise

to be detained

until   is removed from the United Kingdom in pursuance of

Article 8 of that Order.

One of Her Majesty's

Principal Secretaries of State

Home Office

Queen Anne's Gate

.... (Date)

Other titles of related interest

Information Sheets on the Prevention of Terrorism Act 95p

This new set of information sheets explains clearly the rights and obligations of individuals held under the extensive police powers provided by the PTA. The sheets cover:- What is illegal under the PTA; Arrest, questioning and search; Exclusion; Travelling between Great Britain and Ireland; and International Interest Groups.
NCCL 1985. ISBN 0 946088 14 4

Abolishing the Diplock Courts £2.95

S. C. Greer & A. White
The case for restoring jury trial for scheduled offences in Northern Ireland
Cobden Trust 1985. ISBN 0 900137 27 4

Armagh Strip Searches £1.95

An independent inquiry into the strip searching of women remand prisoners at Armagh Prison between 1982 and 1985.
NCCL 1985. ISBN 0 946088 20 9

Use and Abuse of Emergency Legislation in Northern Ireland £2.95

Dermot Walsh.
This important survey of the administration of justice in Northern Ireland describes the continuing abuses of civil liberties which take place under the emergency legislation. It examines arrest interrogation and the operation of the non-jury Diplock courts by analysing the official court records and draws on a series of interviews with people from both sides of the religious divide who have been detained under the emergency laws.
Cobden Trust 1983. ISBN 0 900137 20 7.

Supergrasses: The use of accomplice evidence in Northern Ireland £1.50

Tony Gifford. The results of Lord Gifford QC's investigation into the use of supergrass evidence in Northern Ireland, where many have been charged and convicted, frequently on the uncorroborated evidence of an accomplice.
Cobden Trust 1984. ISBN 0 900137 21 5.

ADD POST AND PACKING: Total up to £1.95: 25p
Total £2.00 – £4.95: 40p
Total £5.00 – £9.95: 75p
Over £10.00: POST FREE

NCCL/The Cobden Trust, 21 Tabard Street, London SE1 4LA

——NCCL——

Information Sheets on the

PREVENTION OF TERRORISM ACT

KNOW YOUR RIGHTS!

- What is illegal under the PTA
- Arrest, Questioning and Search
- Exclusion
- Travelling between Great Britain and Ireland
- International Interest Groups

95p

These new information sheets explain clearly the legal rights and obligations of individuals held under the extensive police powers provided by the Prevention of Terrorism Act.